The Girl Who Lived: A Story of a Resilient Heart

By Destinee Brooke

This publication is designed to provide accurate and authoritative information in regard to the subject matter covered. It is sold with the understanding that neither the author nor the publisher is engaged in rendering legal, investment, accounting or other professional services. While the publisher and author have used their best efforts in preparing this book, they make no representations or warranties with respect to the accuracy or completeness of the contents of this book and specifically disclaim any implied warranties of merchantability or fitness for a particular purpose. No warranty may be created or extended by sales representatives or written sales materials. The advice and strategies contained herein may not be suitable for your situation. You should consult with a professional when appropriate. Neither the publisher nor the author shall be liable for any loss of profit or any other commercial damages, including but not limited to special, incidental, consequential, personal, or other damages.

Book Cover by Destinee Brooke, KDP

First edition, 2025

Table of Contents:

Dedications:

To Mom, who is finally free

To Desiree, who was too innocent for this world

To Sawyer, who I love with a love that is more than love

To the warriors who are breaking the chains of generational curses

Prologue:

I've been telling and re-telling my story to anyone who would listen for as long as I can remember. I don't do it for attention or pity – I've pitied myself enough throughout my life. I also tried to ignore my pain hoping it would go away. I was able to disassociate myself from the events so much that my rendition became the equivalent of re-telling the plot of a somber movie. My story almost always warranted the same reaction of pity with a hint of admiration, not that I was ever anyone worth admiring. I'm still not anyone worth admiring.

I never internalized my grief because it was easier for me to distance myself from the tragedy. I didn't have the skills and tools needed to work through my pain. Though I didn't realize it at the time, based on what I know now, my constant sharing was an attempt to connect with someone and make sense of it. I longed to belong somewhere based on what I'd come to base my entire identity. I was desperate for someone to see my pain, but I was too scared to open up.

The reasons I'm relaying this story to you today are entirely different from those in my youth. I no longer seek to belong; I've found contentment and peace with where I am. Instead, I hope to illuminate the challenges people like me face when overcoming generational trauma. While my story is depressing and heavy at first, I urge you to hang in there because it gets better – there is light at the end of the proverbial tunnel.

I have three things I want to tell you before you continue reading this book, which narrates the series of forlorn events in my life:

First, I want to preface everything I'm about to tell you by stating that I am not searching for pity or sorrow in what I will disclose. Sharing my story has been a way for me to process everything I've been through by mapping and categorizing my experiences in a way that helps me make sense of it all. My goal in sharing my story is not for you to feel sorry for me but to help you make sense of your healing. There are too many people who are hurting. We need to heal, and that takes place one warrior at a time.

Secondly, I must say that not everything I'm about to tell you is my own lived experience. This book is a collection of family stories from various eyewitness accounts, and is not meant to be an exposé. This book is the most complete rendition I have to offer, as the people of Appalachia fiercely desire to separate reality from perception and protect how the outside world views them.

My family grew up in the Appalachian hills in West Virginia, so we are no exception to that desire. There is a lot I do not know about my family's history, and I've grown to accept that.

Lastly, I do not blame anyone mentioned in this book for their actions. They did their best with the tools and skills they were given. Just as I'm learning to forgive myself for allowing my pain to pour over into those around me, I've learned to forgive others for allowing their pain to do the same. It hasn't been an easy process.

My humanness still limits my emotional capabilities. I have to make a conscious effort every day to ensure that I understand people's negative behavior rather than taking offense to it. Instead, I've chosen to extend grace. I came across a quote by pastor Charles Swindoll recently that I feel perfectly encapsulates the importance of extending grace and patience rather than anger and blame:

"Grace... embodies almost every attractive quality we hope to find in others. Grace is a gift of the humble to the humiliated. Grace acknowledges sin by choosing to see beyond it. Grace accepts a person as worthy of kindness despite whatever grime or hard-shell casing separates him or her from the rest of the world. Grace is a gift of tender mercy when it makes the least sense."

With that, I hope you can extend grace to the people in this book, myself included, and understand that all of us were doing the best we could with the skills we had been provided. It takes lots of gut-wrenching soul-searching to acknowledge the depth and breadth of the trauma so that the healing can start.

There is hope on the horizon, and I am moving forward it in faith.

I also hope that if there's anywhere in your life you can extend grace – with yourself for having wronged someone or with someone who has wronged you – I pray my story helps inspire you to do so.

**Characters in this book are based on real people and events, but some names have been changed for privacy purposes.

Accused of attempts to kill child, woman waives hearing

Publication: THE CHARLESTON GAZETTE

Published: Thursday, June 11, 1998

Page: P9A

Byline: Not Available

A 37-year-old Charleston woman accused of trying to murder herself and her child waived a preliminary hearing Wednesday, and Magistrate Kathy DeMarco ordered the case held for grand jury action.

Meanwhile, [Betty] Vance remains free on a $100,000 bond.

Vance is accused of three abortive attempts to kill her 4-year-old child last week.

She is charged with attempted first-degree murder, attempt to kill by poison, and felony child abuse.

The mother allegedly tried to hang herself and her little girl by tying a rope around their necks and attaching it to a hook in the ceiling of her Sissonville area home - an attempt that was unsuccessful.

She then is accused of wrapping a coat hanger around herself and her child, and then inserting the end of the wire hanger into an electrical outlet.

That, too, failed. So the woman is accused of trying to give her child an overdose of a drug believed to have been Valium, then swallowing some of the pills herself.

After the pair were treated at CAMC, General Division, the child was placed in custody of state Child Protective Services.

Chapter One: It Started with Her

West Virginians are often referred to by many different stereotypes and slanders, and that's if we're lucky enough to be acknowledged as a state separate from the "western part of Virginia". When we are recognized, though, we're referred to as *hillbillies, rednecks, creekers, bumpkins,* and *hicks*. While some of the stereotypes might ring true to outsiders looking in, I can't help but feel a need to understand where these labels originated, especially given my family history. That's the thing with these hillbillies and bumpkins, too - they tend to suffer mostly in silence. They are taught from a young age to suppress negative emotions, lest they reveal the dark reality of life behind closed doors to the world beyond. They're also instilled with a fierce desire to uphold and protect the family legacy and honor, even if they project all smoke and mirrors to the world.

For this reason, I will probably never know the whole truth about my family's history – it's been hidden behind shame and swept under the proverbial rug, never again to be acknowledged. The lack of

acknowledgement of the pain inflicted throughout the generations

allows and encourages the pain to be passed down.

Like veins, the creeks and hollers run through the mountains and

hills of the Appalachian region, winding around and connecting

everyone. They mean to offer a sanctuary from the busy, bustling life

that has become popularized and has created an anxiety-ridden

society. They help keep families together and foster a sense of

community and a slower way of life where you really do have time to

stop and smell the roses, and it's not just a colloquialism uttered out of a

half-hearted desire to do so.

Unfortunately, many hollers are also breeding grounds for

secrecy and temptations. Once these things take root, it's a slippery

slope because of the protection of the foliage and the family name.

More often than not, these hollers tend to harbor all of the family

secrets, cupping them within their banks and valleys and holding them

captive, damaging anyone who chooses to stay.

The problem with hollers and the little houses tucked back into

them is that there isn't much awareness of how to deal with difficulties

within families. That's how it all started, at least as far back as I know.

From the outside looking in, no one would ever know. The

mustard yellow of the siding looked inconspicuous enough. The four-pane casement windows exuded a quaint innocence. The carport indicated having had enough for a family in the hollers of West Virginia in the 1960s. The chain-link fenced-in yard seemingly welcomed passers-by to venture up the two steps to the covered porch and take a load off on the pleather couch. The scene looked promising, and anyone would assume that a loving, happy family occupied the walls of the home.

When it was purchased in 1960 by 21-year-old Bennie Edward Hanson for himself and his 16-year-old pregnant girlfriend, the house had the potential to be the perfect family home. Somebody laid the foundations carefully, and every detail of an architect's design came to fruition. Unaware was anyone who had taken such great care to build this house that it would harbor the pain and anguish of a little girl – pain that would leak out and hurt everyone around her.

In October of that same year, Goldie, the woman I would one day call Mamaw (pronounced "Mom-*maw*"), gave birth to their first child - a little girl who would later become my mom - whom they named Betty Ardith Hanson, after her father.

Bennie and Goldie wed the following year, in 1961. Bennie worked on road construction, and Goldie took on the role of housewife and mother, taking pride in her ability to keep a clean home and cook for her family. They had two more children: a girl, Gertie, and a boy, Edgar.

My grandparents took on traditional roles, which rode the line of modern-day sexism.

Somewhere around this time, Bennie, who had already developed a taste for alcohol, began imbibing more and more with each passing day, unable to cope with whatever demons he was struggling against from his own checkered past. He and Goldie had their bouts of physical violence with one another, each of them trying to hold their ground against the other.

They had each brought the baggage of mental illness from their families before them – schizophrenia from Bennie's side and bipolar from Goldie's side. In came as no surprise then when Betty started exhibiting signs of mental instability. Betty would become enraged at the slightest inconvenience - chasing after and threatening harm to her younger siblings.

Then later, when she wouldn't get her way, Betty would try to overdose on Aspirin in an attempt to end the war that waged in her mind. She felt alone even though she was seemingly constantly surrounded by people. Nobody understood just how much she was suffering.

So, it made sense that, when she was just seventeen years old, Betty eloped to Giles County, Virginia, in April of 1978 to marry Ralph Vance. The two had grown up in the same holler right across the creek from one another and had fallen in love—the epitome of a hillbilly love story.

In truth, they were both running from generational trauma and trying to make a new life for themselves while leaving everything and everyone else behind. Their hopes were high, but their sense of self-worth was low. It was a recipe for disaster.

Ralph had his demons with whom he wrestled. Ralph's biological parents, who were also raging alcoholics, traded their young children – both Ralph and his sister, Galena- to Ray and Gypsie Vance for a bottle of whiskey. Others in the community believed that the Vances would take good care of these orphaned children, and Ray and Gypsie formally adopted Ralph and Galena.

While they were church-going folks on the outside, Ray was a die-hard alcoholic who all but gambled his life away in cock fighting when he wasn't at church on Sunday mornings.

Ray talked the talk of Christianity, much like many of the other men in the town, but he wasn't willing to walk the walk. Though they claimed to be Christians, they lived a life driven by sin.

After their wedding, Ralph and Betty felt they'd escaped the prisons in which they'd been raised. Undoubtedly, the change in physical location would also leave behind the memories and emotional and mental distress associated with it. If only.

Betty, for once in her life, was optimistic. She was excited to have someone who loved her, start her own family, and do things better. They moved into a tiny one-bedroom utility building right outside Ray's house. Even still, they were content.

They'd left behind the chaos, pain, and abuse. She finally had a clean slate to make a new life for herself. Ralph no longer had to be around Ray and the violent behavior brought on by his alcoholic tendencies. The old habits of living in chaos and being in constant survival mode would not cease to exist with the simple change in environment and a hopeful "I do" sealed with good intentions and a kiss. They would not be able to outrun the ghosts of their pasts.

Chapter Two: A Losing Game

Neither Ralph nor Betty had been shown a good example of marriage – they'd grown up in emotional and financial poverty. Betty's parents had shown a façade of a marriage behind the smoke and mirrors. Ralph's adoptive father had abused his wife. They'd never learned what a healthy, supportive marriage looked like. The odds were only stacked against them.

The two eventually purchased a tiny home along the slight stretch of road between where they grew up. Betty tried her best to be a good wife and took pride in her duties as a housewife. In the beginning, Betty kept their little trailer spotless, just like her mother had before her, and always had dinner ready for when Ralph got home from work, where he worked on HVAC systems. The two went on to have two daughters, Abigail and Stella, in 1980 and 1982, respectively. Ralph and Betty wanted to give their kids the stability and consistency they had never been allotted in life.

Unfortunately, because they had both grown up in abuse and

drunken chaos, that's all they knew, and it didn't take long for their little fairytale life to erupt into the chaos and violence they were both so accustomed to. The stress of their daily lives, added to the pressure of trying to break generational curses, was too much. They both broke under the pressure of it all. And no one was there to pick up the pieces.

Studies have shown a pattern in girls who grow up and then marry men who are similar to their fathers. This statistic can benefit those with good, loving fathers who love and respect their wives and work hard to provide for their families. However, this statistic does not bode well for those who do not have good examples from their fathers. With the statistics and the sting of mental illness stacked against her, Betty was doomed to fall for someone abusive like her own father had been. Ironically enough, Galena would go on to marry an abusive alcoholic as well, and their son would also go on to be an abusive alcoholic. So the cycle goes on.

Additionally, Betty continued displaying signs of bipolar disorder around this time, which is known for causing severe mood swings in its victims. She could go from a happy, bubbly person so excited to be alive one moment, and then she would erupt in anger because her life felt out of control.

She took out this anger on those closest to her; she would scream at Ralph, cuss at him, and blame him for everything wrong in their life.

Ralph wasn't to blame, though, and Betty knew that. She was scared that she would never outrun her childhood. She was constantly on edge, as was Ralph - they'd not yet felt safe or healed enough to let go of the fight-or-flight response.

She wanted everything to be perfect, and when things weren't going her way, her anxiety got the best of her. She would throw things at Ralph, slap him, and spit in his face because she didn't know how else to communicate with him the turmoil that was raging inside her head.

Ralph had not learned good communication skills either, so he didn't know how to process or talk through the issues that were arising. They were two broken people trying to make it work, but their circumstances forced them to face their trauma and the effects it had on their lives without being given the tools to handle it. With seemingly no other way to cope, Ralph did what his birth father had done before him: he began to drink heavily.

He drank all the beer he could get his hands on, and when that ran out, he drank the cough syrup for the girls and even tried isopropyl alcohol once (before spitting it right back out). He created an endless cycle for himself that involved getting drunk and getting violent.

One particular evening, in a rage during a fight, Ralph was drunk, and he busted out the windows of Betty's car. She took Stella and Abigail to a homeless shelter for battered women that night. Betty asked that the girls keep their stay in the shelter confidential. News travels fast in small towns, and she did not want to draw attention to herself. Goldie had taught her never to let 'em see you cry.

She didn't want to embarrass her mother because she knew how important the family legacy was. The last thing Betty needed at that point was to be disowned by her mother while her life was also falling apart. She was barely keeping it together as it was. The next day, though, Betty ran right back into the arms of the man who had hurt her.

Betty left Ralph multiple times after that. Once, when Ralph was inebriated, Betty scooped her girls up in her arms, flung open the back door, and dashed across the field behind their house in the moonlight, desperate to escape. The crickets and spring peepers promised comfort even though they could not provide it in the given situation. Behind her, Betty heard the echo of a shotgun reloading rip through the tall grass around her. She held her girls close as she hunkered down and ran for the neighbor's house on the other side of the field. Ralph fired shot after shot that failed to hit their target – his wife, the mother of his children.

Breathless from both running and the anxious adrenaline that comes from having her husband shoot at her and their kids, Betty made it to the neighbor's door. She stayed there with the girls that night, but it wasn't long before she returned, hopeful as ever for her happily ever after and desperate as ever to be loved.

Ralph and Betty bought a trailer and moved it onto Reese's property, tucked back in a valley. Ralph, intoxicated yet again, chased Betty out of the house, yelling and carrying on that he was "done." Betty was standing in the culvert driveway they shared with Reese, sucking on a cigarette to help calm her nerves which were on the verge of fraying beyond repair.

Ralph stumbled to the drain, and Betty turned her back, white smoke billowing out of her mouth as the nicotine worked its way through her system, numbing her senses. Just what she needed.

Before Betty knew what was happening, Ralph had smashed the side of her face with a fist-sized rock he'd found in the drainage pipe beneath the culvert. Blood poured down her face as she tried to make sense of what had just happened.

Her world had tilted on its axis yet again. She felt betrayed. Again. He had promised he loved her. He had promised to protect her. His violence toward her was not love or protection.

After that, Betty accepted defeat and knew that she would likely die if she stayed in this marriage. With a throbbing pain in her face where the rock had made contact, she decided to file for divorce. The next day, sporting sunglasses to cover her severely blackened eye, Betty slid the girls into the cold plastic booths of the local Dairy Queen. She told Abigail and Stella that their mom and dad would split up.

Betty was devastated - she thought she had finally left all the despair in the past, and Betty truly loved Ralph as best as she could. And he truly loved her, as best as he could. But their pain was so great that it got in the way, and they just couldn't make it work. She moved her trailer off Ray's property into a trailer park. She was out on her own and tried to tackle the life of single motherhood in a world that was not built for that. She got a job to provide for herself and her girls.

She was hurting and in desperate need of healing, neither of which she knew where to even begin. Betty would not abide by the number one rule in marriage in southern society, thanks to Miss Tammy Wynette: Stand by Your Man. Feeling like a failure in Southern society and expectations, Betty slipped into the first of many mental breakdowns in her adult life.

Schizophrenia is another mental illness that significantly affects a person's ability to function in their daily life. The victim usually suffers from severe and irrational paranoid delusions and hallucinations, among other behavioral issues. The illness usually presents itself in people between 18 and 30 years old. Just like clockwork, Betty had already started showing all the signs of a paranoid schizophrenic with bipolar disorder. After their divorce, though, the symptoms of mental illness just got worse.

Betty was paranoid that people were spying on her. She would hallucinate things that didn't make sense to her, like her father staring into their bedroom window. She would break down into a complete, paranoid and terrified panic, sure that he had come to hurt her.

Betty experienced manic highs where she would spend all of her money on Reese's Peanut Butter Cups, cigarettes, and Pepsi, and she would have depressive lows where she would try to overdose on too many pills or cut herself as cries for help.

In fits of rage over often the most uncomplicated issues, and because she felt that her life was so out of control, Betty began beating her daughters, Abigail and Stella. She was angry at how her life had turned out. Where was her happily ever after, like in all the movies? She had felt on the outside her whole life as she struggled with her bipolar, and she wanted to feel accepted.

She had two children to care for, but how was she supposed to care for them when she fell apart? She didn't feel her situation was fair - she thought she'd been through enough. Something had to give. As many mothers do, Betty felt the weight of the responsibilities that make up motherhood.

Her life felt so incredibly out of control that she craved control of any kind, even in the most minor things - even if it meant sacrificing the emotional well-being of her daughters as she screamed at Stella and Abigail because they didn't fold the towels correctly.

And Betty was so tired of telling them again and again exactly how to fold them. She couldn't understand why they couldn't just do what they were supposed to do, how they were supposed to do it.

So, Betty beat them. She feared that if she didn't, their bad decisions and disobedience would continue, and they would turn out like she had. She beat them in hopes of breaking them. She wanted to beat them into submission so she could have control over *something* in her life.

As she got older, Abigail often fought back while Betty was attacking her, taking swings at her mother whenever she could to save herself. This insubordination made Betty fight back with even more vengeance. She put on boots, kicked the girls, and swung the belt buckle side of a belt at the girls' heads.

Stella and Abigail went to their teachers and administrators at their elementary schools, lifted their shirts, and showed them the bruises. When they told the adults at the school, rather than deal with the paperwork that was sure to come with filing a report, those adults looked the other way. Nobody ever called Child Protective Services or intervened to save them. Her pain was pouring out and damaging relationships with everyone around her.

More than anything, though, she was desperately trying to dampen the pain of feeling unloved with whatever – and whomever –

she could get her hands on. Her village of family, friends, and neighbors stepped in to help. They often took Stella and Abigail in when things with Betty got too tumultuous - so bad she had to be admitted to a mental health facility because she was neglecting her children or threatening to kill herself. But they never reported Betty for abusing her kids. They covered for her and enabled the abuse to continue.

She underwent treatment in the form of pharmaceuticals, and doctors provided an endless supply of toxins to balance out Betty's chemical imbalances. Sadly, no one ever really attempted to get to the bottom of Mom's issues and figure out why she was the way she was.

Sure, her mental illnesses are primarily hereditary, but they're also heavily influenced by risk factors that can send someone spiraling. She was just drugged and sent away with a new prescription after some "observation." Betty was, like many others who struggle with trauma, stuck in an endless cycle that those who suffer from severe mental illnesses go through.

The doctors guess what will work for the patient's mental health and write a prescription to act as a band-aid for the issue rather than digging up the roots of the poison. The patient fills the prescription and starts taking it, anxiously waiting to be magically "fixed" because that's what they've been misled to believe.

And so many of those medications dull the storm of anxiety to the point that they also dull the sunshine of happiness, and people become walking zombies.

Rather than follow doctor's orders and take her medication consistently since she hated the way they sucked the life out of her, Betty was self-medicating any way she could: smoking cigarettes, spending time in bars sipping on a beer or five, and bringing home any man who showed interest in her because she was desperate.

She spent money she didn't have to keep up appearances and fill the voids left by her pain - anything to feel an immediate increase in dopamine because the quick hits of dopamine were the closest thing she could get to true happiness. The reality was that she was more anxious and angrier with life than she cared to admit. Everything was extreme - her feelings of love, lust, anger, sadness - and she felt everything deeply. With her chaotic upbringing came no self-awareness or healthy coping mechanisms. She was trying to run from everything that reminded her of her childhood and the lack of control and security that she experienced.

She didn't realize that, in doing so, she was losing control of her own life and ignoring the problems her trauma was causing her.

They weren't making them go away; they only rooted themselves deeper into her psyche.

Chapter Three: Doomed from the Get-Go

After Betty escaped her abusive marriage, she earned money as a house cleaner for the wealthy in and around the capital city of West Virginia. She beamed with pride, knowing she could provide for her daughters independently. But she was forced to abandon her pride and dignity and sign up for government housing assistance when the landlord refused to fix the broken gas line after Betty and the girls had gone months without heat or a working stove. She moved to an apartment complex called Meg Village, and by this time, she had turned to a more professional job to make ends meet. She got a job at Shawnee Hills Mental Retardation Center in Charleston, West Virginia. This job offered a work program and environment to those who were "societal rejects," as I've heard it referenced.

Eager for love and affection and relentlessly hopeful that something would work out, she must have sensed some promise in Brandon, one of the delivery drivers, because Betty melted when he wrote down his name and number on a sticky note and left it on the windshield of her car. The two were immediately smitten. Brandon indicated that he was still married but that he and his wife were separated and "basically divorced." He told Betty he did have one daughter, Hannah, with his wife, but he didn't want anything to do with his previous family. Brandon promised her he would be the knight in shining armor she'd sought. Betty said she was worried he'd leave, and he said all the right things and swore his devotion to her no matter what life threw at them. Betty expressed her insecurities and worries due to what she'd been through. She'd learned that men's actions were more trustworthy than empty words and promises. Everything changed when two pink lines showed up on the pregnancy test.

People around her found out about Betty's sinful pregnancy and encouraged a "solution": get an abortion and take a used car as restitution. They wanted to cover up the product of Betty's desperate search for love rather than support Betty during this low point in her life. Lucky for me, Betty wanted better for herself and her kids – more than was ever wanted for her. She chose life.

Betty carried on her pregnancy without much support. Her close friend, Debbie Jordan, threw Betty a baby shower at their church. It had been so long since Betty had given birth, and she no longer had the necessities for a newborn.

Betty had to start all over. I was a surprise - a screwball - in her already hectic life. Not many people in her life were willing to celebrate a bastard child. Betty felt, again, so lonely. She was welcoming a new life into this world and felt like she couldn't even enjoy it. Abigail and Stella helped set up the nursery in Betty's bedroom closet. They gently and carefully placed the onesies and socks in their designated drawers, the buttery fabric waiting to slide onto my baby-smooth skin.

As if my conception and gestation weren't laced with enough pain already, Betty labored for two weeks before she delivered.

Early one Saturday morning in September of 1993, Betty called Debbie Jordan and told her she needed to get to a hospital. Her five-foot-three physique doubled over in pain.

After the hospital staff took note of Betty's medical card and the fact that her water hadn't broken yet, they turned her away despite her obvious need for medical attention. The two women hadn't made it very far from the hospital when they turned back around, more resolute in their decision now that Betty's contractions were too close together and she was gasping for breath.

Debbie retrieved a wheelchair for Betty to sit in while the nurses finally checked her in, deciding that she was actually in labor this time. The nurses finally took Betty back to a delivery room with Debbie in tow. They administered the epidural, but I was born before the anesthesia could even begin to set in. She felt like her body was ripping in half. And then, in the early morning hours of September 18, there I was, struggling to catch my breath. Mom's pack-a-day of cigarettes, despite her being pregnant, had done a number on my lungs. I turned blue from lack of oxygen.

The doctors rushed me into the Neonatal Intensive Care Unit, where I was kept on oxygen for a few days until the nicotine and tar worked their way out of my system as best as they could, and I could breathe on my own.

Brandon didn't show up at the hospital. Mom, who had never returned to her maiden name, Hanson, was still a Vance by law. She gave me the last name Vance at birth because she wanted me to have the same last name as my older sisters. Ralph, of course, was never happy about that since I wasn't his child. My birth certificate never listed a father.

The courts subpoenaed Brandon months later, via the local newspaper, for a last chance to claim me. When he didn't show up for court on that given day, the court released Brandon's rights and responsibilities to me from then on out, doing him a favor while leaving me stuck with the transgression. He legally owes me absolutely nothing, and I'm the one left with the heartache of his and Mom's irresponsible choices.

When the doctors released me from the hospital, Stella was so excited to finally have a real-life baby doll to replace the pretend ones she'd been playing with for years. She was 11 years old at the time and treated me with the same care and attention that she had her baby dolls.

Stella took such good care of me: changing my diaper, feeding me, playing with me, and dressing me. This was helpful, as shortly after Mom brought me home, she had another one of her mental breakdowns.

Debbie Jordan took me in to live with her for the three to four months that Mom was in the local mental hospital. Again, Mom catapulted into a rollercoaster of manic and depressive cycles. The stress of the holidays was enough to send her into a downward spiral that usually lasted a few months.

She wanted to afford people the perfect gift, but the government had set her budget since she was on Supplemental Security Income. Her symptoms often started with paranoia and then progressed into a severe emotional range before devolving into paranoid schizophrenic hallucinations.

Someone around her would usually intercept before things got too bad - either Gertie or Mamaw. They would then coerce Mom into getting admitted into a mental health facility so that she could be under constant supervision, and nurses could force her to take her medication to stabilize her. Then, she'd be released into the world to do it all over again.

I spent my first Christmas with Debbie Jordan and her family because Mom was a patient at the local mental hospital. Mom, her love language being gift-giving, made a point to make my first Christmas as memorable as she possibly could. She had Debbie sign me up for the Salvation Army's Angel Tree so I could get gifts from someone – Mom had always equated gifts with affection.

After Mom had me and suffered that first breakdown, everyone around Mom was kind of holding their breath - hoping that things would get better and she would be able to carry on a semi-normal life. They were hopeful that the "third time" being a mother would be a charm and that she wouldn't do the things to me that she did to Stella and Abigail.

They were hopeful that Mom would bounce back and be better than ever. Brandon came around a few times after I was born, and there are a few pictures as evidence. I was only a few months old, but he never stayed, for one reason or another. Around this time, Mom met John, who was also going through a divorce with his then-wife, Judy. His son, Joey, was the maintenance man at the Meg Village apartment complex where Mom lived, but Joey was also living there with his one-year-old daughter in light of his recent divorce. John would come to the apartment complex and visit Joey, and father and son bonded over the pain and heartbreak of divorce.

As is usual for apartment complexes, people congregated outside when the weather was nice and shared in camaraderie and cigarettes. They also used each other's drama and emotional turmoil as a source of entertainment since they didn't have much else to entertain them. Mom got to know John this way, and the two were quickly drawn to one another.

John would go on to be the man I called "Daddy" for most of my childhood and teenage years because he was the only man I'd ever known to be associated with my mom. People also say that John treated me like his own child and was around me more than he had been around for his children.

John was working at Cleveland Fresh Flowers in town around this time. He brought Mom bouquets of the freshest flowers daily; sometimes, he would bring the company van home, the back still full of flowers, and let Mom pick out whatever she wanted. The two loved each other to the best of their abilities.

John had strong Native American Cherokee Tribe blood coursing through his veins, so his overindulging in alcohol came as no surprise. By this point, Mom was still living in fight-or-flight mode, as she'd also struggled to find her footing since childhood. She was also dealing with the pent-up aggression and anger that she had been carrying with her since her childhood.

Neither Mom's nor John's parents loved their children with the unconditional love that parents should graciously bestow upon their children every single day. Neither of them knew what that looked like – they only knew what they'd seen.

John drank heavily to deal with his trauma and stress, and he tried and failed to hide it from Mom. She would ask him to go to Eddie's Market to get some milk, not knowing that Eddie's Market had also expanded to include Eddie's Bar—just another one of the weird things that happen in small towns. John would stop, grab him a beer and then the milk, and head home.

Mom, of course, could smell the alcohol on John's breath upon his return, and a fight would break out. Terrified, I tried breaking them up by wedging myself between them. Mom would often yell at me and then toss me to the side so that she could resume her business.

Mom and John pushed and slapped each other. Sometimes, they would venture outside and return with scratches and bruises on their elbows and knees after a while.   Once, I remember when I was about three or four years old, John choked Mom out for something, probably fighting over who smoked the last cigarette.

I walked into the living room, and Mom was lying on the floor with bright orange puke in her hair. I thought she was dead, and I asked

John about it. I wanted to tuck myself into the safety of her torso. I tried

to run to her and save her. Before I could do anything, John scooped me

up in his arms, and we went to a bar where I sat on the side of a pool

table while he played with his drunken friends.

The country music blaring from the jukebox and the cloud of

cigarette smoke overwhelmed my senses. John went to the bar to get

away from Mom's aggression when she got overwhelmed about money

or cigarettes or having to take care of me. Mom, refusing to be left,

would often follow John to the bar.

One night, in the middle of winter, when I was about two or three

years old, Mom was headed to the bar where John had gone to get

away. He had taken their only car, so Mom set off walking.

I was dressed in a thin summer dress while Mom carried

me. Abigail, about sixteen at this time, pulled up beside us, her breath

and car leaving vapor in the cold air, and she was entirely shocked by

how little clothing I had on. She unzipped her coat and wrapped me in it

so that she could share some of her body heat with me.

She put me in the car with the heat blasting and held me, with

the coat still around me, right up against the heating vents to try to trap

the heat to warm me up because I would not stop shivering. Mom just

continued her walk to the bar to find John, leaving me in Abigail's car to warm up. She was seemingly indifferent to the fact that I even existed, much less that I had almost frozen to death.

By this time, Abigail, who had been living with Mamaw Goldie for a few months, was pregnant with my niece, Harper Faith. Abigail was still in high school, but that didn't stop her living situation from being disrupted when Abigail turned down the "deal" for a car. So, Abigail moved in with her much older boyfriend and the father of their child, Kyle. John met Kyle at one of the local bars, as Kyle was not only a frequent customer, but he also frequented local karaoke nights and competitions, where he beat out many of his competitors.

Around this time, Mom and John were moving from the apartment complex at Meg Village and into a trailer in Pine Valley Trailer Park. John, who was drunk per his modus operandum, was driving to the trailer to drop off some things late one night. He missed his original turn and thought he could make the turn on the entrance ramp from the opposite way.

His car went over the hill with me in the backseat. Miraculously, I walked away without so much as a scratch. Abby, who always seemed to be driving by at the right time, stopped when she recognized the car. She pulled me and my car seat from the back and put us both into the back of her car. She knew that John was already going to get in trouble for drunk driving, but she didn't want him to get in trouble for reckless or child endangerment. John went to jail again that night, and Joey bailed him out as usual.

When we finally moved to the trailer park, and Mom slept a lot and refused to get out of bed to get me something to eat, I would take matters into my own hands. I pulled out the drawers in the kitchen and used them to climb up onto the counter and then climb on top of the refrigerator to get some cereal. I loved to sit in front of our little television in the living room, watching Sesame Street or Country Music Television music videos so I could sing and dance along to my favorite country songs.

When there was nothing else to eat, sometimes I would walk down the road to visit someone we knew to get something. Nothing happened from what I can remember, but the neighborhood wasn't exceptionally safe.

People often say that it takes a village to raise a child. I had a collection of guardian angels around me, protecting me. Mom's close friend, Neva, often loaded me up in her car in a Cabbage Patch Doll car seat and took me to the store to get something to eat. Stella, who was in middle school then, saved her school lunch or her friends' lunch and brought it to me in the afternoons so I would have something to eat. She changed my diaper as soon as she got home from school, which would be sagging down to my knees because Mom hadn't bothered to change me all day. Debbie still took me in sometimes when

Mom neglected me because she was too depressed.

Chapter Four: When Her Pain Hurt Me

Mom often stopped taking her medication, insisting that John was poisoning her or mixing up her medications. This paranoia was just a symptom of her schizophrenia. The paranoia, of course, would lead to Mom spiraling out of control since she would already be in a fragile mental state. Once, when I was four years old, Mom gave me away. Her car insurance was through one of the local insurance providers, so Mom had gotten to know them well enough over the years. Their good reputation within the small town preceded them, which was enough of a safety measure for Mom. She dropped me off at their place of business and left, stating that she could no longer care for me.

The couple who ran the insurance agency had children of their own, and they were both worried about how I would influence their children since they weren't aware of all the details of my upbringing thus far. The owner of the agency, Pearl, hired a nanny to take care of me full-time.

Mom must have told someone about dropping me off because one family member or another picked me and brought me right back to Mom.

Mom acted out, hurting anyone she could, out of spite. On that fateful day when I was four, only a few weeks after she'd tried to give me away, Mom had gotten upset with Goldie over not being able to get to the post office to pick up her monthly checks.

Later that day, Mom, John, and I were riding down the road in their white car. They had started arguing, and Mom decided she'd had enough. She got out of the vehicle and unstrapped me from my car seat. The next thing I remember is us being back home in our living room, and Mom was manic. She kept insisting that she wanted us to go to heaven, stating that she was tired of this world and all the hurt, pain, and fighting and just wanted it all to end – and wanted me to go with her. The way that she was describing it and talking it up, I got excited. We were going to go to heaven.

We'd gone to church before, so I understood what heaven was and knew it was a paradise. I pictured Disney princess castles in the clouds and streets of gold like I'd heard about in church. Mom reminded me, too, about the pearly gates to heaven, and I imagined myself walking through them and God welcoming me into His Kingdom.

As we were getting ready for our trip to heaven, which I thought would be akin to some kind of magic carpet ride like the one I'd seen in *Aladdin*, I was anxious about finding something to take to heaven.

I couldn't decide which one of my many Barbies and dolls to take, and I was worried about leaving some of them behind, never to see or play with them again. Mom assured me that heaven would have all the Barbies and dolls I could imagine and that I wouldn't need to worry about taking any of them. My fears eased a bit, so when Mom handed me my purple sippy cup with silver stars to take, I trusted her and didn't think anything of it. I never could have known that she had crushed up her Valium and mixed it with my drink. At this time, I didn't yet understand death and what it meant to "go to heaven."

Mom, who had entered her room, returned with a wire clothes hanger. She hung the rope over the joist in the living room. She scooted the couch over so that it was under where she had placed the hanger. She then instructed me to climb up on the arm of the sofa and to put my neck into the rope.

She was going to pull the couch out from under me. I remember getting frustrated because I couldn't quite reach to get my chin up over the bottom of the rope, and I was having trouble standing up at this point, thanks to the cocktail she had given me.

Mom dragged down the bottom so it took on a more diamond

shape so that I could reach it better. I didn't understand how this was supposed to get me into heaven; all I knew was that my mom wanted me to do it, and I trusted her. It was my mom. Of course, I trusted her. I could tell she was getting frustrated, and I felt guilty for letting her down.

I don't remember anything else from that night, possibly because of the Valium she gave me to try to make me overdose. Reports have also claimed that she wrapped a wire clothes hanger around me and stuck it in a light socket to try to electrocute me.

Sometime during all of this, she must have phoned for help. I don't know why, since Mom had never before reached out when she was hurting any of her daughters, but for some reason, she reached out to call her friend Neva in the midst of trying to kill us both.

"Where's Destinee?" Neva asked, frantically?

"She's in bed, asleep," Mom answered.

Mom had already admitted to giving me Valium, so Neva knew that my life potentially hung in the balance. Neva didn't know if I was asleep in my bed, or dead.

Neva, yanked out of her peaceful slumber, hung up and called emergency services to come and save me before it was too late. Neva tried to distract Mom, telling Mom to put on a pot of coffee to keep her hands busy and no longer hurting me. She waited for the paramedics to arrive before driving over, scared of being the one discover my body. After a few minutes, she drove straight over to Mom's house. Neva is Mom's cousin, so the two grew up together as most cousins used to.

As the two of them grew up, Neva was around for some of Mom's lowest moments. She indicates that Mom didn't intend to follow through with her antics; it was more of a cry for help to get someone's attention.

Maybe she needed money, and people weren't listening to or taking her seriously, so she'd do something drastic and crazy to prove to them how badly she needed money. What happened that night was no different, even though the stakes were higher than ever.

"Where's Destinee?" Neva asked when she walked into Mom's house. The police and paramedics were with Mom at the dining room table, and she pointed to me as I stumbled and swayed in attempts to walk down the hall.

Neva sat with me on my bedroom floor while I was trying to play with my Barbies. I swayed back and forth and slurred my speech. The paramedics asked Neva if this was normal behavior for me since she had been around me so much up until this point in my life. She indicated that it was not normal behavior and that I was usually bubbly, playful, and happy, not this inebriated shell of a little girl sitting in front of them.

The paramedic asked what had happened and what my mom had tried to do. I pointed to my neck, said, "Mommy tried to hang me on the wall like a picture," and told them we would be angels. I pointed to a picture of Abigail at her prom, which was on my dresser, when I talked about the angels. I thought, in her sparkling midnight blue dress, that Abigail looked like what I imagined angels looked like.

When I lifted my neck to show them, they saw the ligature marks on my neck and Neva's heart broke for me all over again. The paramedics transported me to the hospital, where they pumped my stomach of all of the medication Mom had given me, and the doctors monitored me to make sure there were no lasting side effects. Mom insisted that I not be placed with anyone in the family, even though Abigail was eager to take me, as was Gertie and her husband Dale and even Neva.

I never really understood, and neither did anyone else, why she didn't want me to be with someone I knew, especially after I'd gone through something as traumatic as this. One would think that she'd want me to have familiarity and stability.

Because she'd been upset with Goldie that day, Mom didn't want me to live with anyone who would give Goldie access to me. Again, it was all for spite – not my best interest, not because she loved me.

As dawn broke the next morning, Stella started the final day of her 10th-grade year. Nobody wanted to upset her and cause her to fail her finals, so they kept the news from her until she got home from school. She moved in with Ralph during this time because Mom was in jail for about a month before Goldie bailed her out, pulling whatever strings she could with the connections and money she had.

Social workers for the Department of Health and Human Resources placed me in a foster home with Tammy and Kevin Sneed. Though I couldn't quite identify the feeling then, I now realize that I felt overcome by this intense sense of grief at having lost something vital – something that I would never again get back. Not only had I been robbed – of any sense of peace, equilibrium, true joy, and normalcy. I felt like I'd lost my mom.

She didn't die, but I lost the stability that comes with living with one's birth mother. I lost the ability to turn to the one person I was supposed to be able to depend on.

I lost the ability to trust her. I lost my innocence and my childlike wonder and view of the world. The reality of this world and the evil that corrupts it was too much for my young eyes and mind to take in, but it forced itself upon me, and I relented. I had no choice.

Chapter Five: Looks Can be Deceiving

I was their first foster child, as Tammy and Kevin could not have children of their own, and I seemed to adjust well to the change. I was amazed at the size of their house because it had two floors, and I'd never been in a home with stairs before. I would climb up the stairs and sit on my butt, sliding down the whole way. I would sing and dance my little heart out to Shania Twain's "Man, I Feel Like a Woman" and "Don't Be Stupid." I wasn't showing any signs of having been through something as traumatic as I had been, and Tammy and Kevin did their best to give me a happy home. I was a bubbly, passionate child who seemed to love life. They took me to the dentist for the first time, even though the American Academy of Pediatric Dentistry suggests that children should have their first dental visit by 12 months. I got glasses, too; sitting in front of the TV for hours when Mom was still in bed had damaged my eyesight.

Tammy gave me money, and we would go to yard sales every weekend during the summer, and she would let me pick out whatever I wanted. I got to have an actual birthday party and got all kinds of gifts

and all the Barbies my heart could wish for.

That Halloween, I dressed up as Belle from *Beauty and the Beast,*

and Tammy even made my hair look like Belle's in the movie. I felt like a

Disney princess in my yellow costume gown and was waiting for my

happily ever after. Kevin's brother, Steve, had a girl my age named

Chelsea, and we immediately became best friends. She shared my love

for Barbies and dressing up.

It's a common misconception among my family that Tammy and

Kevin were trying to "replace" Mom in my life and negate what she

meant to me because they wanted me to call them "Mom" and

"Dad." More than anything, they were just trying to stabilize me. I had

been through a horrible and traumatic experience that had utterly

rocked my world. They were trying to do what was best for me, not

replace anyone in my life. Having gone through all that I did, my mom

trying to kill me was so normal to me – as normal as the fact that the sun

comes up each day. It's just how it was, and that's just how my life was.

On the outside, I seemed happy and well taken care of, and just looking

in, you'd never know anything was wrong.

Tammy and Kevin had made plans to adopt me, as they both felt

that I was adjusting well and was responding to treatment and play

therapy with a woman named Cherie Crowder. Gertie and Dale were trying to get custody of me, and Abigail and her husband, Kyle, were also trying to get custody of me. Mamaw Goldie was pressuring Gertie and Dale to get custody of me so that they could slip me back under their wings and keep the family secrets hidden away again from the world. An inspector went to Abigail and Kyle's trailer and noted they didn't have running water then. Their living situation automatically took them out of the running for custody; the odds were against them anyway because Abigail was so young – she was only 18 years old and was already raising their two little girls, both under three years old.

Tammy and Kevin got involved in a brief custody battle with Gertie and Dale. Tammy argued that I would lose the progress I'd made in healing and that moving would only make things more difficult for me. As usual, the court system just wanted to do what was easiest for the paperwork side of things when, rather than go through with the long and tedious adoption process, they chose to transfer custody to Gertie and Dale. It also helped that Mamaw Goldie paid off the right person to get what she wanted.

Gertie and Dale's daughters, Delilah, a year older than me, and Gabriella, a year younger, welcomed another playmate with open arms. Delilah was still in school for the remainder of her kindergarten school year when I moved in with them. Gabriella and I spent days watching cartoons and playing in the yard, so we got close.

When I brought all of my belongings to Gertie and Dale's, they didn't want Delilah and Gabriella to get jealous of my toys and clothes, so they hid them in storage. I asked about my belongings multiple times, especially wanting to play with my paper dolls of my favorite Disney princesses, but I was told that they were in storage. I never got any of them back and was told, years later, that the storage building that they had been in had burned down.

I felt like I needed to present this persona of being happy and brave in order to appease everyone around me. I feel like people kind of forgot I was suffering. I hid my pain as best as I could to keep them comfortable - to keep it from billowing over and hurting or affecting those around me. I was worried that my pain would drive them away, too, and they had even fewer reasons to stay than anyone else who had already left. Not that my severely damaged brain could have articulated that at that age, but looking back on it, I'm able to see it for what it was.

I visited with Mom several times at a nearby local fast food restaurant. Gertie and Dale took all three of us girls there to have dinner with Mom back when all the fast-food restaurants still had playgrounds for kids. Mom wanted me to sit and spend time with her, but Delilah and Gabriella begged me to play with them. I couldn't resist. Mom was fighting with Gertie to have our visitations somewhere more private for her and me so I wouldn't be as distracted. Eventually, my caseworker set up weekly supervised visitations at a counseling center in town.

On Wednesdays around lunchtime, Gertie picked me up from school, and I visited with Mom. A play therapist was always down the hallway from our playroom, listening to ensure everything was going well. Still, she didn't hover and make us uncomfortable during our visit or feel like we couldn't be ourselves, which we appreciated.

I loved these visits with her. She always said, "I love you as big as the sky." She loved on me whenever I wanted, burying her face into my neck and laughing in my ear, which always tickled and made me giggle. She played whatever I wanted to play, like with Barbies and puppets, marble ramps, and unique art projects, and she'd often talk about God and how important it was for me to lean on Him. I was too young to understand, and she was just trying to ensure I had something good to cling to amid my despair.

She gave me her full, undivided attention during that time, and I loved it because I didn't get that anywhere else. She loved me strictly for who I was. I could count on her to accept me no matter what. Even though she was the one who had hurt me the most, my mom was still my safe space.

Mom would often call and want to talk to me, but no kid, especially those growing up in the 1990s and before, wanted to be stuck in one spot via a landline talking to a dull adult when the whole wide world was outside and I had yet to explore. I know she meant well, and she was trying to connect with me and make up for the fact that she and I didn't live together. Dale and Gertie tried to help with this.

For the first year or so, they made it a point to record me anywhere we went, whether it be to the zoo or the beach, with one of the old hand-held video cameras, and they would have me give a shout-out to Mom and John. They would then give those tapes to Mom so she could feel like she was getting to experience my childhood with me and wouldn't feel like she'd missed out on so much. She couldn't be there to send me off on my first day of school, take me on vacation, or go to the park, so Gertie and Dale tried to document those moments for her so she felt included.

I also took turns visiting my sisters on the weekends; one weekend, I'd see Abigail and her family, then I'd have a weekend off at home, then I'd visit Stella and her husband, Rory, followed by another weekend off at home. On my weekends with Abigail, I would play outside and in the creek with her daughters, Harper and Sadie. We would watch scary movies at a much younger age than we probably should have and dance to Britney Spears's music.

Rory and Stella took me to church on the weekends they had me, and then we went to Rory's parents' house for lunch. Rory's older brother and his wife would also come over, and we would all sit down to a home-cooked meal courtesy of Rory's mother, a fantastic Southern-style cook. The kind that tastes so good, you know it will put some meat on your bones. While I loved being surrounded by people I loved and staying with different families, it was hard on me. I didn't have a firm foundation on which to establish my identity since neither of my parents was there to help me. Anyone and everyone else around me so easily influenced me.

I was becoming an amalgamation of each version of myself I'd had to create to fit in with the various families. I'd learned to cover up the few things I did know about myself and who I was because they were too painful to look at. Rather than inconveniencing people with the pain of what I'd endured, I became who they wanted me to be instead.

I used to talk so much about how much I loved going to Stella's that it must have gotten on Gertie's nerves. She claimed that "Snelly" - her nickname for Stella, which was, I assume, supposed to be a blended name using snooty and Stella – was brainwashing me. They didn't like Stella – they said Stella thought she was better than everyone else in the family. None of which was true, of course. Stella was just breaking generational curses.

My teachers tried placing me in a Gifted program because they saw my potential. Gertie and Dale refused to allow me to be in those programs because they didn't want Delilah and Gabriella to feel inferior.

I stopped wearing my glasses since the pretty girls in my class bullied me so much, and my eyesight deteriorated.

For Christmas, Mom would sign me up for every church toy drive and Salvation Army's Angel Tree so she could give me all the gifts my heart desired. That was *still* her love language.

I told her about seeing a Brandy Barbie doll in stores that I liked and that I liked her music. On the next visit, Mom would have said Barbie in hand. I now realize she probably went without a lot because she wanted to replace her lack of presence in my life with presents and gifts.

Delilah, Gabriella, and I spent our childhood riding horses, four-wheelers, and bikes. Dale's air compressor and pneumatic stapler made a familiar sound as we played outside.

He ran an upholstery business in one of the many buildings on his property. We would go to Movie Star on Fridays to rent movies for the weekend, our hands full of free popcorn bags as we eagerly awaited watching our films.

We went to the library and participated in the summer reading programs. Uncle Edgar would come over on Fridays, drink beer with Dale, and play board games with us girls. He had nicknames for all three of us. Delilah's was Podge because that's what she used to call everything when she was younger, including one of her favorite foods at the time:

peaches. Mine was Slim because of how skinny I'd been when I was younger due to malnutrition on Mom's behalf. Gabriella's was Buffy because she used to say "buff" instead of "both."

I wish I had been placed in intensive therapy to help me process the tragedy that I'd been a victim of or to help me cope with any of the trauma that I had endured, or the trauma of being currently separated from my mother. I think a lot of people believed the problem would disappear if they ignored it long enough. I wish that were true.

The images of Mom trying to get me to hang myself played in my mind on repeat. I was worried I'd forget if I didn't keep replaying it, and thus, history would repeat itself. I also wondered what I'd done to deserve this. I asked: *What was wrong with me that made Mom want to kill me and not my sisters?* I convinced myself that I was defective, and that was why all this bad stuff had happened to me.

Gertie constantly had the radio playing in the house, always set to one country music station or another. One song, Doug Supernaw's "I Don't Call Him Daddy," would come on, and I would break down crying. It's about a parent who has to go long periods without seeing his son, and the son doesn't care about what he gets to do with his dad; he's just happy he'll get to see him. That song resonated with me, even as a six and seven-year-old.

The song explains that, though there is someone else in his life, nobody can ever replace the dad's place in the son's life. I felt like my mom would always be my number one, even though I was with a new family and inherently knew that I would never be loved or treated the same. Nobody would be able to replace her, even though my pain was because of her. So, I'd hide behind the placemat or anything close, the tears sliding down my cheeks, and wait until the song was over. I learned at an early age to cover up my pain rather than allow it to make others uncomfortable.

I searched for comfort in sad music and movies to feel like I had a good reason to be upset. Movies in which characters lost their mother triggered me growing up, and yet I watched them over and over again because they helped me not feel so alone. I could find an emotional connection in the characters I had not experienced in real life. Some of my favorites were: *Life Size, The Land Before Time, Hope Floats, Dumbo, The Hunchback of Notre Dame* and *Tarzan.* I realize now, looking back, that these were symptoms of PTSD.

I tried to pretend everything was okay, and so I went. I faked it until I made it. I focused my negative energy on being a bouncy, energetic kid to prove to everyone around me that I was, in fact, okay. I kept telling myself to be positive, thinking that if I said it enough, I would believe it. If I believed it, it would have come true, right? It never manifested itself, not really.

A façade that all was well was the only thing that manifested, which led me and everyone around me to ignore the infection that my trauma planted inside me and was now festering under the surface of the mask that I was showing to the world and myself.

Chapter Six: What Did You Expect?

I hadn't learned to communicate hard feelings or how to have uncomfortable conversations, so I shut down.

Nobody sought help when, at just nine years old, I stated that I wanted to kill myself because I couldn't get a Barbie. I was on vacation one summer with Rory and Stella at his parents' house in North Carolina. They'd moved there after they felt led to start a family business selling modular homes.

During one of our stays, we'd gone to a local Walmart, and I was perusing the toy aisle, as I did any time I could because I was obsessed with Barbies. I picked out a Barbie I wanted, and Rory and Stella said no because I had too many dolls already. They offered to get me an art kit or a book. I crossed my arms in the middle of the toy aisle and huffed that I wanted to kill myself. It came down to the fact that I didn't feel understood or heard; I just couldn't vocalize it then.

I used to fantasize about the fact that killing myself would actually make people care about me and love me, which I didn't feel like I could receive or was worthy of receiving in life. For me, playing with dolls was more than just having a pretty representation of who you aspire to be one day. It was about vicariously living out the life and providing the stability I needed for my dolls. It was therapeutic for me in a way. My life was so out of my control and so far from the norm that it felt nice to be the one to provide an everyday life for my Barbies.

Nobody helped when, in fifth grade, I got jealous of a boy because he liked my best friend instead of me. I was tired of always being chosen over, so I called my friend, Morgan, every bad word I could think of. Worse still, I wrote them down on paper with my other friend, Ashleigh, while we were on the bus home. Morgan and I weren't talking, and then I gave said paper to Morgan when we made up.

I was trying to apologize for saying and thinking awful things about her. I thought giving her the paper would give her power and make her more likely to forgive me. Her mom worked for the school in one of the special education rooms, so Morgan showed it to her mom, who showed it to the principal.

Our fifth-grade teacher, Ms. Elkins, sent me to the principal's office the following day. She gave me her signature *I'm not messing around* look that all of her students had come to fear: she looked up at me and to the right of me through a furrowed brow. I knew I was in trouble.

When I got to Dr. Martin's office, she pulled out the familiar piece of paper that had been folded and unfolded many more times since I'd last seen it. The writing, though, the horrible words I'd written - *bitch, whore, slut, asshole, faggot* - (that last one courtesy of the friend who helped me write the list; I'd never heard that word before) were evidence of my doing. I couldn't deny it.

My heart sank to my stomach, and I hung my head in shame as the blush of guilt and embarrassment crept over my chest and face. Our principal told me I would eat lunch outside her office and could not participate in the traditional Halloween parade around the school's parking lot. A letter stating what I'd done would also be sent home and needed to be signed and returned to school Monday morning.

Stella and Rory were coming to my class's Halloween party this year and were going to watch me in the parade. I was heartbroken at the thought of them thinking I would be a bad influence on their little boy, Spencer, who was three then and whom I had come to think of as my little brother.

I tried to convince them to get custody of me, but I worried they would no longer be interested in me or no longer love me if they found out the truth. I kept my mouth shut during the party and tried to be on my best behavior so they wouldn't suspect anything.

Afterward, when Delilah, Gabriella, and I loaded up in Dale's truck after school that afternoon, I realized I'd forgotten to grab the wretched letter from my desk, where I'd hidden it. I told Gertie and Dale that I had a crucial letter in my classroom that I needed to get or I'd get in big trouble on Monday. Dale left to get it, and the girls, Gertie, and I held our breath in anticipation for him to return. They didn't know what was coming. I held my breath because I did.

Finally, Dale came stomping back to the truck, red from the neck up. The letter flopped in the wind, already removed from its envelope. Delilah and Gabriella asked what was going on, and Dale, through gritted teeth, just said he'd talk to me when we got home. I hid my face in the window to my right, and I silently cried the whole way home because I was scared of what was to come.

I was so ashamed of my actions. I should have known better. I was just trying to do the right thing and apologize, and I still got in trouble. I worried that they wouldn't want me anymore.

Anticipation and anxiety grew the entire ride home down our windy road, and by the time the gravel of our driveway crunched under the tires of the truck, I felt like I was going to throw up.

But nothing happened that evening. Nobody said anything to me, and everything proceeded as usual. The following day, as I was playing in my room, Gertie told me she wouldn't be punishing me for what I'd done because she could tell how guilty I felt. She believed that was punishment enough. At the time, I heaved a sigh of relief. And she was right - I did feel shameful and guilty. I was afraid people would think I was a bad person and they wouldn't love me anymore.

Nobody said anything when I tried multiple times to run away because I hated my life, and I felt like I didn't fit in. Delilah and Gabriella had this beautiful wavy hair; mine was wild and unruly with curls. I always felt like an outcast; I was the troublemaker and the one with too much energy.

I lived life wide open, constantly searching for the next thrill to distract me. I didn't think twice about playing in the mud and the creek until Gertie reprimanded me for getting too dirty. In old home videos Dale recorded of us at the beach, Delilah and Gabriella sit still, playing in the sand, and I run around in circles. I was the one who was too brave and took too many chances, often leading Delilah and Gabriella to follow me.

For example, when I climbed to the top of the pine tree in the yard, I waved, covered in sap, to Gertie and Dale from the top of the tree. Delilah and Gabriella were still only a few feet off the ground, trying to figure out how I got up so high. I was reprimanded and told to get down, and Delilah and Gabriella were discouraged from doing as I did.

Or when I pushed my bike to the very top of the steep gravel driveway that ran up the back of our property and felt like I was going to take flight as I rode it down. The wind was whipping my hair and making it hard to hear or breathe, but I grinned the whole time as I gained speed like never before.

Delilah and Gabriella stared, open-mouthed, as I finally slowed to a bumpy stop at the end of the gravel path. Then, they grabbed their bikes and started the hike up the hill.

It only took them a couple of times to do it before Dale, who was doing upholstery work in one of his sheds, noticed and yelled at us for being so reckless. "It was *her* idea," either of the other girls would say, pointing at me, and I would be the one who was put in time out or made to go inside.

And so it went, on and on. I felt like I couldn't be myself. I felt a deep desire to be seen – really seen – for who I was.

I felt smothered to fit into this tiny little box to be what I deemed acceptable, but I had so much energy, passion, and zeal - some would now be quick to diagnose me with ADHD. I lived loudly, constantly seeking attention and thrills in hopes of being seen. Gertie insisted that I was too much - too loud, too rambunctious, too energetic, and too passionate. I felt like I was suffocating.

I packed my little pink duffle bag that I used on the weekends away with my sisters and planned my escape. It wasn't difficult. The original backdoor to Gertie and Dale's double-wide was now my bedroom door, as they had built a bedroom/playroom just for me. They put in a new back door to which I now had easy access, perfect for any subtle escape. I couldn't leave without telling Delilah and Gabriella goodbye, though, and they threatened go running to Gertie and Dale. I never got any further than just a few feet out the back door.

Nobody ever asked why I was trying so hard to run away. Nobody tried to figure out why I was so unhappy. They labeled me as too difficult, too impulsive, and too troubled. Dealing with me had exasperated my guardians. I was hurting, and the trauma that had taken root in me was growing more and more every day, rooting itself into every aspect of my life.

I was doing all I could to seemingly hold my breath to keep the pain from leaking out and hurting those around me, but the pain sometimes got to be too much for me to handle.

When I was eleven years old, during one of our last visitations at Process Strategies, before Mom stopped showing up, she dropped the bomb on me about my dad. Until that point, I hadn't considered who my dad was. I had always assumed it was either John or Ralph somehow. I did, after all, share Ralph's last name.

But John had also always been there. I had already started burying any feelings I didn't understand about myself or the world around me because it was easier than asking questions and then getting answers I didn't like or being given no answer, just as I had learned to.

Mom told me very little, only stating that his name was Brandon and that he was my real dad. He had another family, a wife and a daughter named Hannah. She also said Brandon didn't want me, and that's why he went back to them. I just nodded and returned to playing with the hand puppets.

Meanwhile, I felt like a black tunnel of darkness and despair was about to swallow me whole. I felt hollow. Mom looked at me expectedly, as if waiting for some more significant reaction. I didn't say anything. I just sat and stared off.

I realized that this meant, too, that I didn't have the same father as Stella and Abigail. The last thing I felt I had to cling to in terms of belonging was ripped out from under me. I didn't belong with them either, not really. I was sure my heart was going to break right in two – the pain was suffocating.

Mom went on to pat my leg and tell me that even though Brandon had never been a father to me, I always had God as a Father. Internally, I rolled my eyes at her, my pre-teenage girl attitude already in full swing because I was trying to process the fact that my dad had abandoned me. He had chosen someone else over me. I'd grown up until this point, watching movies and television shows glamorizing a father-daughter relationship that I would never have. He had known about me and chosen that I wasn't enough to make him want to stay.

And the next thought that came right after that was: *If you're not enough even for your dad, you'll never be enough for anyone, Destinee.* That was what played on a loop in my head for almost two decades.

Rather than allow myself to get further upset or worry about it, I refused to let myself think about it. I shut down emotionally and detached myself from it as much as possible.

I didn't think anything else of it. I didn't understand why I couldn't or wouldn't react then, but now I realize it's a defense mechanism. Nobody had protected me growing up, but I was getting pretty good at defending myself.

The pain and heartbreak of not being able to grow up with and be raised by my mother had already done enough damage to my psyche. The one person I wanted to live with – my mom - was not allowed to have custody of me, and yet I could not understand why she would want to kill me.

This one revelation about not being loved by my father would wreak havoc within my entire being. The idea that I was defective took root in my psyche that day. Everyone else around me had parents who loved them and were present, except for me. I didn't understand why mine didn't. I didn't know why I had been abandoned and discarded by the two people who had created me.

I didn't understand why everyone else got to experience the unconditional love of their parents while I was got "leftovers" from everyone simply because I wasn't their offspring - their flesh and blood. That's not to say I don't appreciate their sacrifices and efforts, because I absolutely do. But it's never the same. And that's what I needed.

I had also formulated this fantasy in my head that, had Brandon stayed, Mom wouldn't have tried to kill me. He would have provided her the stability and love that John couldn't.

Mom wouldn't have wanted to kill me; she would have showered me with the love I so desperately needed. There was no way of knowing if reality would have played out that way had Brandon stayed, but it gave me a glimmer of hope, which I clung to like a lifeline.

Shortly after this, Mom got paranoid that our play therapist was spying on us during our visitations and was reporting things that she said and did to my social worker. Gertie had picked me up from school and driven to the counseling office two weeks in a row, waiting for my mom, who never showed up.

She didn't bother to call either. I lived for those visitations because Mom always made me feel as if I was all that mattered to her in the whole world in the moments that we were together. So, when she stopped showing up, I realized I couldn't depend on anyone. I started to feel like I was inferior. I questioned my inadequacies - was I just not enough? What was so bad about me that neither of my parents loved me enough to stay or to want me? I felt like both my parents had abandoned me. This despair, mixed with the spiral that is already pubescent hormones, was a perfect recipe for disaster.

I had felt a shift of bias/unfairness toward me as I lashed out a few times while staying with Gertie and Dale. I told myself I was defective and unlovable, and that's what I became. Granted, I wasn't an easy kid to raise, especially given my childhood thus far and the fact that it wasn't being dealt with or acknowledged.

Because I was so insecure and could easily see that Delilah was the favorite, I often made it a point to draw attention to her flaws and uniqueness and poke fun at them with Gabriella. I was so desperate for love that I convinced myself that if I could make them see her flaws, they'd think I was better and choose to love me more instead. Delilah was always very sensitive and gentle, so when her feelings would inevitably get hurt, and she would tell her parents, I would get the brunt of their anger. I got spanked and made to sit in time-out more times than I can count.

I had become obsessed with following, keeping up with, and reading about various celebrities. I looked up to them as role models and wanted to dress and look like them.

I was back to comparing myself, which was ingrained in me, and my obsession with celebrities like Britney Spears, Hilary Duff, Lindsay Lohan, and the Olsen twins didn't help. I would never look like them, but I was impressionable and insecure, and that's precisely whom the media and celebrities feed on. I wanted to look like them and be like them because I equated the adoration these celebrities received from their fanbase with love and acceptance, and that's what I was so clearly craving and missing. The idea that I would never be worthy of anyone's attention and love was drilled deeper into me every day.

I started to hate living with my aunt and uncle – it wasn't necessarily anything that they did or didn't do. I couldn't put my finger on exactly how or why I felt so suffocated, only that I knew that if I didn't get out soon, I was going to drown - devastatingly collapse in on myself - and there would be no saving me. It was my negative inner dialogue and self-hatred that convinced me I was a burden to them and that they hated me

I had started to beg either of my sisters to take me in at this point. The legal age for children to choose with whom they want to live in West Virginia is fourteen, and it has been for some time. I was only twelve and knew I wouldn't make it.

Abigail had three daughters and an older stepdaughter from Kyle's previous marriage. She had moved into a concrete block house up

Crack Rock Drive, right across the creek from where her father, Ralph, still lives. She was barely making ends meet as it was. Another mouth to feed would have been too much, and I would have had a big responsibility. She was dealing with too much.

Stella and Rory still only had Spencer at this time, as Stella had been diagnosed with thyroid cancer at the young age of 22 years old. She had to undergo intensive radiation treatments on top of numerous surgeries. She was under strict orders not to get pregnant, as the chemicals would have been dangerous to any potential children.

So, Rory and Stella petitioned the court for custody of me. It was a long, brutal fight that I was not aware of at all until I came home from school three days before my thirteenth birthday. Gertie came in and told me that the judge had granted Rory and Stella custody of me, and they would be there to get me soon.

While I was eager to get away from them and feel like I belonged somewhere, I couldn't help but also feel a ping of sadness in the back of my mind at the thought that I was so easily dispensable. Little did I know that they were about to get so much worse.

Chapter Seven: Time for a Change in Scenery

When I moved to Rory and Stella's on September 15, 2007, I had a fresh start, and I was hopeful that, with their lead, I would follow God more, get involved in church, and things would magically fix themselves. They led me to get baptized, and I was involved in the youth group full-time. Gertie and Dale dropped off almost a dozen full trash bags a few days after I left. I went through the bags, choosing to take a step toward maturity and discard all of my Barbie dolls.

Among my dozens of Barbie dolls and the stench of cigarettes that clung to my clothes like a lousy habit were other items that Gertie and Dale had decided to discard. I guess it was a way for them to "stick it to me" for leaving. Now that I was living with Rory and Stella, they felt betrayed and hurt – like I didn't appreciate their efforts. That wasn't the case at all; I simply needed more space and air to breathe. At this point, I was just trying to adjust and find my home. I wanted to feel like I belonged somewhere.

At first, things were good. I had grown to believe I owed every family I lived with an easy time since they sacrificed so much to take me in. I had my thirteenth birthday party at the local ice rink with many friends from school. We spent the afternoon attempting to ice skate, falling on our butts, and laughing. I was thrilled - so much so that it made me uncomfortable. I felt like an imposter - I wasn't used to feeling this much love, nor did I think I deserved it.

One of my presents from Rory and Stella was a cell phone - a Sony Ericson flip phone. Stoked to have a cell phone, I also had this sense of anxiety in the pit of my stomach at the thought of growing up and what that meant for me. It's like I could sense the impending doom that was to come. I was also in no rush to get too comfortable in this new house with this new family.

From my experience, everyone had abandoned me, and with Stella's cancer, I figured her days were numbered already. I kept everyone at arm's length, unwilling to let anyone get close to me. Closeness with others, to me, equated to getting hurt and betrayed. I had to protect myself from allowing that to happen again. I'd been through enough already.

Stella and Rory both had excellent jobs, and Stella got me clothes from the mall, which was the first time I'd ever gotten clothes from one of the high-end places like JCPenney's and Kaufman's (before it became

Macy's). She also bought me real-wood furniture from a fancy, high-end furniture store. I'd never gotten new furniture before. I got a new desk and dresser combination set with a hutch and a bed with storage drawers underneath.

At Gertie and Dale's, we'd gotten clothing vouchers from the government to help pay for school clothes. We went to more thrifty places like Gabriel Brothers, Value City, and Kmart for our clothes. Don't get me wrong; I am all for a good deal. But in the early 2000s, name brands started to matter for the younger generation, so not having those brands made me an outcast and "lesser than" by default. I'd never fit in with the popular crowd, which wouldn't have been too much of an issue, except I'd felt like I didn't belong or fit in in any area of my life. In my naivety, I was grasping at any tangible thing I could to feel like I was enough to belong *somewhere, anywhere,* even if that was to belong to a group made up of acquaintances who were quietly judging me on so many other aspects of myself than just my clothes.

Because of my troubled past, I connected more with my peers who also had troubled pasts or those who came from lower-income families. These kids didn't have motivation or support from home, so they didn't apply themselves to school. In my desperation to fit in, I, too, stopped applying myself in my classes. My group of friends who refused to apply themselves academically widened, and before I knew it, my entire friend group consisted of unmotivated - for lack of a better word - losers.

Pain and the ability to share and connect through that pain draw people together, and that's something I've always been good at. They were hurting, and I was hurting, and I was drawn to that kinship of spirits like a moth to a flame. I stopped caring about my grades and started spiraling into depression. I carved a heart on the inside of my right ankle using a mechanical pencil because I wanted a scar tattoo like I'd seen my friends do. I started self-harming by doing the same thing to my wrists. I was too scared to use anything too sharp or do anything that would cause any real damage, but I still wanted it to hurt, and I wanted to fit in with my friends who were also doing it. I was desperate to belong somewhere, that I became a chameleon – intent on blending in and fitting in however I could.

Chapter Eight: But Some Things Never Really Change

Stella noted that I was not practicing good menstruation hygiene, so she talked to me about the importance of regularly changing feminine products, no matter what type. Mom had barely covered the basics during one of our talks when we were still doing visitations. Gertie had asked if I'd had any questions about feminine hygiene, and I shook my head. I knew so little that I didn't know what questions to ask.

What should have been an easy conversation about feminine hygiene turned into an awkward situation of me hiding and being embarrassed. I cringed at the thought of even *talking* about menstruation because Gertie had led me to believe that puberty and sex as a whole were off-limits topics.

What's more, I was so incredibly self-critical – never feeling like I was enough or assuming no one would accept me for who I really was – that I couldn't bear the thought of anyone else criticizing me.

I crumpled under the pressure and broke down before finally accepting the lesson she was trying to teach me. I'd never learned to communicate about difficult and uncomfortable topics. I did not handle criticism well because I had never had uncomfortable conversations or been confronted. My trauma had left me full of self-doubt. Instead of seeing it as an opportunity to grow, I took it as a personal attack and immediately got offended. Stella expected me to be much more advanced and independent that I'd ever been at my aunt and uncle's, and I struggled to assimilate, which led to many heated arguments between Stella and me. We were clashing. I wasn't fitting in.

They took it upon themselves to teach me how to do basic chores and be accountable for myself. What should have been an easy lesson on vacuuming the carpet turned into a fight.

What should have been a simple explanation about how to rinse the shampoo and conditioner from my hair correctly turned into a meltdown on my end. It wasn't that I was trying to be difficult. I was hurting so badly that my ego, my sense of self, became as fragile as glass. The smallest of criticisms wreaked havoc on my mental stability, which wreaked havoc on everyone around me. I grew up before texting was popular, and very few kids had phones in middle school.

To communicate in class, we passed notes, unbeknownst to most of our teachers. I quickly figured out which classes were apt for note passing and which ones were not. In the prime note-passing environments, I went haywire and focused on passing as many notes as possible without the teacher noticing. I don't ever remember doing an assignment. All I remember is my notes. I had started quite a collection in the bottom drawer of my desk at home since the documentation of my communication with my peers had amassed quite an accumulation. I sometimes pulled them out and re-read them, reminiscing about the conversation. Most of them were about whichever boy I had happened to have a crush on that week.

One evening, Stella knocked on my door. I had locked it to have some privacy while I re-read my notes. Assuming she would see my notes and make the connection of wasted class time, I panicked and shoved them all back into my drawer. I hurriedly ran to the door, my palms filling with sweat.

"What was all that noise?" she asked me, suspicion written all over her face.

Guilt-ridden and scared of what she'd do if she found out I'd wasted my class time passing notes instead of doing my work, I murmured a quick *nothing* as I moved in front of the drawer to block it.

My behavior didn't fool her and was indicative of nefarious behavior. I pressed my back into it, hoping to make it somehow disappear into the wall behind it. She tried pulling me away after I refused to move away from the drawer. I jerked my arm away from her and glared up at her, hoping to intimidate her enough to make her leave me alone. She called Rory shortly after that, exasperated and unsure how to proceed safely.

After quite a dramatic stand-off, I headed for the kitchen. I was already messing things up and was scared that her view of me would change when she learned I passed notes in class. I worried it was going to make her stop loving me.

I lunged for a knife, and my hand landed around the knife block. Stella, who was already on the phone with Rory and had been for a while until this point, shrieked, "SHE'S GOT A KNIFE!" into the phone.

I hadn't realized how that must have looked for her. I wanted to explain or sputter that it wasn't meant for her, that I was only desperately wanting to end my own life. I wanted to slice at the skin and bleed out into nothingness before she saw me for who I was and decided I wasn't worth loving. Instead, I stood there frozen, the knife extended in my shaking hand.

Her hazel eyes bulged, and she gripped the phone with white knuckles. I eased the knife back into the block, realizing my mistake only a second too late. I surrendered, and she and Rory read the notes I'd hidden together. They were appalled not only at how many there were but also at the content of some of them. Not that I fully understood any of the sexual references that may have been in any of them, but their presence was still worrisome.

I'd learned that the best way to get attention of middle school boys was for sexual purposes, and I equated that with love. As desperate as I was for attention, to be seen and loved, I made it my mission to get as much as possible.

I was mortified and could only think about how much like Mom I was turning out to be or how I imagined others saw her - as this crazed lunatic. That was the first time I'd ever heard Rory yell at me after he got home from work that day. He lectured me for my behavior, for scaring Stella, and for putting Spencer in danger.

I tried to please them and earn their love, but I always seemed to mess things up, no matter how hard I tried. I was too anxious and on edge, impulsive, and not nearly insightful enough. Rather than accepting responsibility and recognizing that I was the problem, I blamed it on everyone else. My insecurities couldn't take any more blame.

Shortly after moving in with them, I told Stella that Mom had told me about my real dad, and Stella commented that I looked like him. I hadn't even considered what he'd looked like, to be honest. His existence was so abstract and nonpictorial to me until then that it wasn't something I'd thought about. He was simply a name that I'd developed a distaste for: Brandon.

Stella stated that I had Brandon's eyes, and I immediately decided that I hated my eyes because they connected me to him. She went on to tell me that Mom probably had some pictures she could show me. Mom handed me a little olive-green photo album the next time I saw her. Confused, I looked at the front cover, which showed a picture of a baby covered in tubes and IVs. Mom said that picture, and the next few pictures after it, was of me right after she'd had me. I'd had to stay in the hospital for a few extra days so the doctors could help me heal from the damage I'd suffered at the expense of Mom's cigarette habit.

Mom told me that the pictures of Brandon were in the back of the album, so that's where I flipped, the plastic picture covers sticky with residue left behind by years of smoking. The first picture was of Brandon, with his dark brown hair cut into a mullet and a thick, bushy mustache typical of men in the late 80s and early 90s.

He was lying on his side on a dingy-looking couch, smiling at the camera, his green eyes shrinking with his smile like mine always have. I turned the page as it crinkled, the yellow and burnt orange aged nicotine tar caked on the corners of the pages, and I saw a picture of Brandon with a little girl sitting on his lap. I immediately knew it was Hannah, and I immediately started comparing myself to her, trying to figure out what it was about Hannah that made her more worthy than me.

Mom often called, trying to reach out and connect with me;

usually, she just rambled on for a few minutes before running out of steam, and then she'd breathe loudly into the phone receiver. Years of smoking had done some severe damage to her lungs. I wasn't one for sharing my feelings, so I never really said much to her. Mom took it personally and was so upset that she told me she no longer claimed me as her daughter. She spent my fourteenth birthday that year at the beach to get back.

I had gotten so used to her making me feel extra special on my birthday that her lack of acknowledgment hurt. She said she loved me. I wasn't exactly sure what love was since I hadn't had many good examples, but I knew enough to know that this wasn't it.

Chapter Nine: Did I Ask for This?

I was still visiting Abby on some weekends, and her daughters and I would stay up late watching movies - *Titanic* and *Ghost Ship* were some of our favorites. I would lie beside Harper in her bed and talk to her about anything and everything; the television light was the only thing that illuminated the darkness. We would talk about how badly we wanted our own Jack Dawson to come and sweep us off our feet and, to quote Rose Dawson from the movie in her old age, save us "in every way a person can be saved." I wanted so desperately to feel safe and feel like I belonged. Those moments with her were the only things that illuminated the darkness in my life during this time. Those nights saved my life, and I feel guilty knowing that my mental stability depended so heavily on a girl three years my junior.

Abby's daughters, Harper, Sadie, Amelia, and I would often commute to her house and Ralph's house, and I had begun to look to Ralph to be my "Papaw Bub" since that's what Abby's girls called him.

In the summer, we would take a break from swimming and run

across the creek over to "Papaw Bub's" to raid his kitchen for snacks or run up the hill behind his house to play in the woods. Ralph treated me like one of his own, just as he always had. When Stella and Abigail were growing up, Ralph often let them pick out toys, clothes, and diapers for me when he took them to the store.

During these summer trips to Ralph's house, the girls and I would burst through the door of his trailer, our bathing suits still dripping wet from the water. I'd filled out my bikini top more since I was older than the other girls, but I was innocent enough not to think anything of it, especially in front of an older man like Bub since I trusted him.

That winter, though, something was different. Ralph hooked a little sled to his four-wheeler and pulled us around in the snow. The girls and I laughed until we almost peed our pants as Ralph did donuts in his yard and made sharp turns that nearly dumped us out of the sled. We held on for dear life, not caring that the snow had soaked our clothes.

Afterward, we all piled through Ralph's front door, shivering from the cold, our fingers numb and our cheeks cherry red. The girls had their room in his trailer, so they picked out some dry clothes from their dresser that they changed into.

Ralph let me borrow a pair of his grey sweatpants until my

sopping-wet jeans got out of the dryer. While we sat at his dining room table, sipping our hot chocolate, I showed Harper how comfortable and warm Ralph's sweatpants were on my still-numb legs. Harper suggested I hug him and thank him, so I did. He was in his bedroom, piddling with something, so I hugged him and thanked him for taking care of me. He held the hug longer than necessary, but I thought nothing of it. Maybe he was happy to be appreciated, right?

The next day, when we crossed the creek to play in the snow, Ralph suggested he ride us up the snowy hill on his four-wheeler. We were all excited to see all the pretty snow. Then Ralph indicated that only one of us could go at a time since we couldn't all safely fit on the back of the four-wheeler, especially going up such a steep incline. I volunteered to go first since I never got to ride on four-wheelers much, as Rory and Stella didn't have one.

I hopped on the back, hanging tightly onto the rear cargo rack, and Ralph started our ascent. The four-wheeler rumbled and vibrated comfortably and familiarly beneath me.

When we were only a few feet up, I got this sinking feeling in the pit of my stomach that questioned Ralph's intentions. I asked myself if I trusted Bub as much as I should since I wasn't related to him.

Nothing brought on these thoughts; they just came out of nowhere. I remember feeling anxious and worried as we chugged up the hill. My stomach was in knots, and I was shivering, but not from the cold of the January chill.

Just as I started to process where these random thoughts and feelings originated, Ralph stopped the four-wheeler on a flat part of the hill. The sudden silence dragged me out of my thoughts, and I returned to the present. Ralph turned around to face me and asked if I could give him another hug like the one I'd given him the day before.

I wrapped my arms around his waist from behind him, and he leaned back into me. He looked back at me and asked if he could have a kiss. Bile rose in my throat out of fear and disgust. I offered him my cheek as I leaned forward, and he swerved to try to put his lips to my mouth.

As a tear rolled down my cheek, I turned my face away so he wouldn't kiss me. The fear I felt was on the verge of suffocating me as Ralph asked me if I'd ever watched a "porno," to which I replied no. I was so naive that I honestly wasn't even sure what pornography was.

I knew it had something to do with sex, but even up until that point, sex in my mind was very intimate and beautiful. I had never imagined the sick, disgusting sex acts that people become addicted to and desensitized to through porn.

I knew enough, obviously, to understand that it meant sex, so I knew, in a sense, what he was asking. In my head, I imagined him dragging me off of the four-wheeler, forcing me down onto the piles of decaying leaves and wet snow, and hurting me and or killing and leaving my body here if I didn't comply. I prayed for the ground to swallow me up. I prayed for God to protect me. I didn't know how to escape this, so I said, "I'm cold. Can we go back down?" By this time, I was shaking uncontrollably from fear, so it was a believable lie.

I remember Ralph sighed loudly to indicate his frustration before he turned the key in the four-wheeler's ignition, and the all-terrain vehicle roared to life. A twinge of guilt passed through me for being an inconvenience – at letting him down in some way, even though this was not at all something that I wanted to participate in. We turned around and started back down the hill. The descent pressed the front of my body to his back, which, again, made bile rise in my throat.

I was now disgusted with this man and how he could put me in such a situation as to try to coerce me to have sex with him. I used the cargo rack to pull myself away from him so that no part of my body was touching his.

I even went out of my way to ensure my feet did not contact his calves. He told me not to tell anyone about this, to which I agreed. I was afraid to say no. I feared what he would do to me and was desperate to appease him to escape this situation as quickly as possible.

After what felt like an eternity, my frozen and numb hands

cramping from holding me away from Ralph, we got to the bottom of the hill. I jumped off the four-wheeler and sprinted down Ralph's driveway and up the road to Abigail's, choosing to forgo the quicker and easier creek passage altogether. When I got to Abby's, I burst into the front door and ran upstairs to Harper's bed, crying. I was terrified of what could have happened to me, thankful to God that nothing had, and in disbelief that Ralph would do that. I trusted him to protect me.

Abigail came up, concern etched on her face, to check on me. I was reluctant to tell her at first because I was scared that Ralph would try to hurt me somehow. He did, after all, only live right across the creek. It would be easy. He had told me not to tell anyone, and with warnings like that, there was typically an accompanying and unspoken threat.

Scenes of the possibilities of what would happen to me if I disclosed what had just transpired to Abigail flashed through my head. They were on a reel, moving too fast to pinpoint each situation, but the intention was clear.

Still, she pressed me for more information. I told her what had happened. I couldn't make much sense of it because I didn't fully understand it. I felt so betrayed.

She called Stella and told her, and they were both surprised that their dad would do something like that, as he'd never done anything like that to them or Abby's girls, who were all bursting through the door asking what happened to me. Kyle asked Ralph what happened to me, and Ralph's face got red, and then he just said he wasn't sure.

For months after that, I woke up in a sweat, barely able to catch my breath because I was having a nightmare related to Ralph. It was almost always the same: he was driving his truck further up the holler, and I was either in front, running from him as he drove toward me, or in the truck's bed, stuck there, as he sped around the turns in the road. Either way, the intention was evident, just as it had been in real life. I was trapped and at his mercy, just as I had felt when I was on the back of the four-wheeler with him.

When I think back on it and the psychology behind being scared, that's what makes a good horror movie. It's the not-knowing. It's filling in the gaps in the story on your own with the most diabolical scenario you can that makes a good horror story.

That's what I was doing in my head every night for months after I'd wake up from said night terror: filling in the what-ifs of each scenario with the worst possible outcome.

And each time, I'd wake up wondering the same thing that society asks of rape victims: *had I done something to lead him on? Had I done something to make him think I wanted that? What did I do wrong?* I felt shame at having apparently and unknowingly given Ralph some signal that made him think I wanted him.

I had begun to think that I was undeserving of God's goodness. All this pain, and I had nothing but scars and battle wounds to show for it, except for a growing list of people I thought I could trust who had let me down severely. I couldn't understand why I felt like God had abandoned me despite His saving me from being sexually assaulted. Stella and Rory put me in Christian therapy, where I attended only a handful of sessions. I heard what everyone told me: God loves you and has a plan for you. I'd heard it so often that I could regurgitate it and let the ideas reside in my mind. I didn't believe it though, not really. I wasn't listening.

I was still hurting too intensely for anyone to reason with me successfully. I was involved in the youth group at my church - I went to the youth group every Wednesday and Sunday evening, and I was in church every Sunday morning.

I was desperate for God to save me, but I didn't trust Him enough to let Him save me. I didn't trust anybody, but I was scared of where this road I was on would take me.

Chapter Ten: Looking for Love in All the Wrong Places

Throughout my life, I've made various attempts to fill the voids left by the trauma and neglect I'd endured. Mostly, those attempts came in the form of boys because I was desperate to be loved and to be connected to someone through my pain. I gave my heart away to anyone who would take it. I'd grown up surrounded by this idea that women were only worthy if they were sexualized or seen as objects. In my desperation for attention, that became the ideation by which I lived my life.

By the time I reached middle school, I'd already had a couple of boyfriends, but they'd both been in fifth grade, so they didn't count. A few months after I moved in with Rory and Stella and the little glow-up, I attracted the attention of a few boys in my class, one of them being a good ole boy named Daniel.

I shared my first-ever kiss with him before catching my bus

home at the end of the day. I did so in the most nonchalant, unromantic way possible. I grew up having this idea drilled into my head that a girl's first kiss was supposed to be this earth-shattering, gut-wrenching, earth-stopping, life-changing thing. Mine was not. It was a quick peck given in passing without thought, and I remember thumping my way up the bus stairs and sinking into the seat, disappointed. That was it? It was supposed to be magical. Nothing at all felt magical about what had just happened. It was pretty uncomfortable because his stubble kind of stabbed into my lips.

Most girls would have gone home and gushed to their moms about having experienced their first kiss. At least, that's what they did in all the shows I watched. But I didn't have a normal relationship with my mom, not enough to open up to her about something like this anyway. I was, again, so programmed to think that talking about boys and anything "grown up" was taboo and embarrassing, so I kept Daniel a secret.

Then, when I realized my inability to disclose that I was in a relationship with my guardians also meant that I wouldn't be able to talk to Daniel on the phone or do any of the typical couple things because I felt I had to keep him a secret.

I didn't need to; in reality, Stella and Rory would have supported and encouraged me and given me good advice. It was just in my head, and I was worried Daniel wouldn't have their approval. In some ways,

I was still stuck in this four-year-old mentality where boys have cooties.

The next day at school, I told Daniel that he and I couldn't be together because my dad didn't want me to date. I lied, of course, because I couldn't bring myself to own up to the fact that I caused the hurt now welling up in his eyes. He talked to one of my best friends about it, and later, when I ran into him in the stairwell between classes, he called me out and asked me why I lied to him. I gulped away the guilt, my heart racing at the thought of being late to class and being called out on my lies. I stopped in my tracks, waiting for him to elaborate more.

Daniel explained that he had talked to my friend Felicia after I broke up with him, and she had explained to him that I didn't live with my dad or I didn't have a dad or something along those lines. I heaved a sigh of relief as I explained my unique situation: "I don't have a dad, no. My sister and her husband just got custody of me, and I just didn't want to have to explain that to you."

I cushioned the guilt that threatened to close in on me for hurting him and lying to him again by telling myself that at least there was partial truth to that.

I *had* just moved in with my sister and her husband, but still, nobody had prevented me from dating as I had claimed.

By the end of my seventh-grade year, I had started the first of many spirals to come. I was dangerously and pathetically insecure and so desperate to feel loved. Sound familiar? I would spend class time passing notes instead of taking notes and completing MASH possibilities for my future instead of my assignments. My grades had dropped tremendously because of it. Stella and Rory were so done with me that they paid for me to attend four summer camp sessions for three different summer camps that summer.

Three of them were Christian camps, and one of them was an adventure camp for rich kids. I had fun, don't get me wrong, and I'm grateful for the experience, but every experience was filtered through a lens of self-hatred. I felt I'd already blown my shot of fitting in with this family, too. I began to have this negative internal dialogue that I was terrible, I screwed up everything, nobody would ever love me, I was worthless, and I would never fit in anywhere.

I hated myself. I didn't respect myself. My circumstances had planted the seed of self-loathing, but by now, the poisonous vines had made their way to my internal psyche - right where the enemy wanted them - and I was on a fast path to destruction. This sense is the only reason I can give for the actions I will disclose to you.

My eighth-grade year saw the revolving door of boyfriends, each lasting a shorter period than the one before. The plot was the same: some boy would show interest, and I would make the first move, desperate to reel him in before it was too late. I knew they'd run away if they saw me for who I was - this broken little girl just wanting to be loved by anyone. Then, we met up between and during classes to hold hands and kiss. I'd learned that physical affection was the best way to get boys' attention. They would break up with me after they felt me up and kissed me a bit. The sentiment was always the same: you're too much - too clingy, sappy, and needy. I was not subtle at all in showing my desperation to be loved. I had become a laughing stock.

My eighth-grade year went out with plenty of tears shed among my friends and me as I went to a high school out of the district to pursue a better education since the high school in my district was known to produce students who were not of the best quality.

Rory and Stella put a lot of pressure on my education and academic success as if that was going to magically save me and erase all the hurt and pain I'd endured. I felt like I couldn't live up to their expectations. Not as severely as I was hurting. Rory and Stella thought it would be in my best interest, wanting the best for me.

Summer came and went, and I went into ninth grade with my self-esteem at an all-time low. I spent hours in front of the full-length mirror in my room, pulling my hair straight with my straightener, my hair sizzling. I caked on makeup to make myself look better than I felt I did. I didn't feel I had much to offer any man other than my looks. I had already come to realize that I was too damaged to be worth anything.

Nobody would ever love me if they could open up my heart and see the trauma that had taken root there, festered, and grown to take over my whole personality. I felt like my body was all I had to offer that was worth anything.

I walked into George Washington High School, and it was like something right out of Taylor Swift's song "Fifteen." I felt so small and wanted to stay out of everyone's way. I had grown up in small towns tucked back in hollers. This new school was full of kids who grew up privileged and wealthy but, most notably, from happy homes.

I again felt stuck in a place in which I did not fit. I had never learned to feel secure and safe in any place I'd been, and this school was no exception. The school had lecture halls, rotating class schedules, and off periods that enabled students to go off campus. It was physically the largest school I'd ever been in, and was intimidating. I got lost trying to fit in, and my grades suffered significantly.

I didn't have a group of friends who took me under their wing to protect me from the junior and senior boys who saw the first-year class as new hunting grounds. So, nobody was there to warn me when I got scooped up by one of the junior boys on the football team during one of my off periods. He led me on a wild goose chase through the labyrinth of halls, teasing me with the pencil he had taken from me. I wasn't doing anything productive when he walked up to me.

I was simply doing it in my notebook again – I should have filled it with notes from my classes, answers to assignments, and reminders for upcoming tests filled with doodles. Nothing kept me rooted to my seat, and I floated along the hallways as I followed him to a secluded spot outside the lower gym doors. I felt so disconnected from myself and from the situation as a whole as he roughly grabbed at my body without asking. I didn't say anything either when he pushed me to my knees on the cold, hard tile while simultaneously pulling down his zipper. The sound was deafening in the closed quarters.

I didn't want this. I squeezed my eyes shut, my hands clammy and shaking, and tried to make everything disappear. I was mortified. Terrified. I knew nothing about fellatio other than a few whispered and giggled words I'd heard from my friends, and even then, my knowledge was minimal.

I knew the words, but I didn't understand the actions. So, I felt violated and dirty, but I didn't resist, and I didn't say no. I did nothing to outwardly indicate that there was a severe mental, emotional, and spiritual storm that was raging inside my conscious and my heart. I knew this was wrong. Just like I knew this was not love. I knew this was nothing good and pure. Amid my internal storm, though, I felt a flicker of electricity in the pit of my stomach. It was just a flicker. As cheap as it made me feel and as wrong as I knew it was, I would keep returning for more.

So, I did. We developed a schedule during our shared off periods - Felix would walk past me, and I would follow him to our spot under one of the side stairwells. I liked feeling wanted, and I subconsciously equated that with love. I didn't think about the fact that he was just using me. I didn't think or care about getting caught, failing high school, or ruining my future. I didn't think about that because I was desperate to feel validation. I was so desperate to feel loved - the unconditional, heart-wrenching, life-changing love that parents usually share with their children and that I had gone without my entire life.

One chilly Monday in October, he passed me in the cafeteria, and I knew that was my cue. I wasn't feeling up to it, as I was tired. Stella and Rory constantly lectured me at home because I did not get good grades.

The revival at church had wrapped up the previous Friday, and I had gone to the front, gotten down on my knees, and quietly asked God to help me stop living for the world. My heart wasn't in it, and I wasn't ready to be changed yet, but I was still asking. But I knew enough that the trajectory I was on was dangerous, and I was scared. I'd learned to keep everything in, not ask for help, and not admit defeat or take responsibility. Even if nobody intentionally taught it, this was how I'd learned to deal with uncomfortable and difficult emotions.

When we got to our usual spot under the stairwell, I sensed something was different with him. He didn't hesitate to ask for more, not at all. I hesitated in my answer. All I'd learned about sex was that it brought babies and STDs.

"Do you have protection?" I asked, assuming and hopeful I would take care of the issue and could walk away. If he didn't, then I would be off the hook. That's what I told myself anyway.

"Yeah, I do in my locker. I'll be right back." He answered, his voice thick with wanting. And off he went. I should have walked away then. I should have come out from under that stairwell and never looked back. But I stayed. And even when it got awkward to wait there, I stayed. Even when someone dropped a note through the small space between the wall and the landing above me that said: "You shouldn't be down there", I stayed.

I ventured out long enough to ascend a few steps to sneak a peek at whoever left the message, only to find that no one was there. And still, I stayed. I'd always thought of sex as this beautiful connection between two people that was sacred and intimate. The small space under the stairs offered none of that. Needing that attention, I moved our backpacks into the small space to provide some padding. Still, I feared when he returned with the little foil wrapper.

I wanted to scream at him to leave me alone, but my vocal cords felt raw. Then, the side door to the stairwell opened, and in came the principal and at least two of the vice principals.

"What the hell is going on here?" gasped the principal, taking in the scene. My heart was thumping in my chest so hard it reverberated throughout my whole body, both from nerves and relief at having been saved from myself.

I had never been more relieved or mortified in my fifteen years. I wanted to die right then and there instead of making the short but excruciating trek to the office to dole out my punishment.

The administrators chose to kick me out of the school. They decided that because I was out of district and this school had a reputation to uphold and a specific clientele they were looking for, I was not welcome back at the semester. And I was given yet another example of how boys are trouble.

Chapter Eleven: But wait... There's More!

That evening, at home, Rory and Stella gave me an oxymoronic, almost speechless lecture, unable to find the words to articulate their surprise and disappointment in me. I couldn't either. They were shocked at my behavior and wanted to know where this came from. All I could do was shrug. I didn't bother offering up an explanation except to assure them that *nothing had happened.* The operative word *yet* hung heavily in the air. Of course, they didn't believe me. But, just like every other uncomfortable feeling I'd felt in my life up until this point, I pushed the shame and guilt aside, and I didn't let myself feel it. I was just numb. I forced myself not to care about what they were telling me to protect myself from getting hurt even more. I'd given up on relying on others to protect me or believe in me. I put up walls and shut people out to defend myself – isolating myself emotionally.

After the initial shock wore off, Stella lectured me about how I was doing everything wrong and how much of a disappointment I was. I couldn't put into words the reasons why I was doing this.

Exasperated, she sent me to stay with Abigail for my 10-day suspension while she tried to figure things out at home. Abigail, wanting to teach me a lesson since I had proven promiscuous, made me get up at 5:30 with her to get her girls ready and off to school. She wanted to show me what life would be like if I continued down the path I was currently treading. She was disappointed in me but was not judgmental nor belittling like Stella tended to be toward me.

In the midst of all of this, I knew that I had messed up. Badly. Irrevocably. Rather than make it right, I refused to face what I'd done. I had been in a constant state of fight or flight my whole life, so I did what I did best: I ran. I decided to stay with my best friend, Eleanor, who attended George Washington High School outside the district as I finished the semester. I would like to tell you that I finished the little time I had left without a hitch. I want to tell you that I learned my lesson and made better choices. But I didn't.

For Thanksgiving that year, Rory and Stella left me to fend for myself. When I called a few days before to see their plans, they told me they'd traveled to North Carolina to spend the holiday with Rory's parents and siblings.

I didn't know Eleanor well enough to be comfortable spending Thanksgiving with her extended family, so I convinced Abigail to let me spend Thanksgiving with her and Kyle's family.

Even though I knew I deserved it, my heart broke at the realization that Rory and Stella had given up on me. The semester ended, and I endured a very awkward Christmas at home. I spent the last few days of Christmas break at Abigail's because I couldn't stand the looks of disappointment that I got constantly at home. Harper, Sadie, Amelia, and I played in the snow until our fingers were numb. We slid around on the frozen creek, laughing until we peed our pants. We danced to Mariah Carey and Soulja Boy Tell 'Em. We gave each other makeovers and then stayed up late watching scary movies. It was one of those days you wish to wrap up and tuck away to cherish forever. Once I got home, Rory and Stella dropped the bombshell of what would come next.

It was late that night when Stella and Rory came into my room. Spencer was already asleep in the room next to me; he didn't need to bear witness to the scene that was about to unfold. They sat on my bed, my twin mattress sinking beneath their weight. My heart sank right down to my stomach with it. They went on to explain to me that they had made arrangements for me to go to a "residential treatment facility" in Tennessee. George Washington High School indicated I was no longer welcome there, as the school had been out of my district. Going there had been a privilege, and I'd blown it.

They explained that I would stay there for at least a few months until I could get myself "under control." They said we would meet some staff members from the treatment facility, Mountain Youth Academy, tomorrow morning so they could transport me to the facility.

They asked me if I would be okay until then and if they needed to take my door off to monitor me - suggesting that I would run away as if I had anywhere to go. Nobody wanted me. My ears were ringing so loudly that their voices were mere muffles. I shook my head slightly in shock as I tried to process what was about to happen, and they left me on my own devices.

My heart hurt - physically hurt - in my chest. The ache was so intense that I thought I was going to suffocate on my pain. I didn't want to run away because I didn't want to hurt anyone else. I didn't want to ruin anyone else's family. I didn't want to be abandoned by anyone else. I didn't have anywhere to go anyway. Nobody wanted me. That much had been made evident, as this experience, again, passed through the lens of self-hatred. I'd burned all my bridges. I was fifteen, and my life had fallen apart more times than I could count. My fragile heart could not handle it. Rather than risk any more hurt, I just wanted to die. I begged and prayed for God to take me in the night. I convinced myself that, once I was dead, people would finally love me. I would finally stop messing everything up.

I wanted to die more than I wanted to be alive. I fell asleep that night in a puddle of tears while I silently begged God to kill me and

wondered why He'd bothered to spare me in the first place.

Chapter Twelve: Welcome to Crazy Town

On January 19, 2009, I woke up to a fresh blanket of snow on the ground and was disappointed that I was still alive. I packed ten changes of clothes, per Stella's instructions, and some toiletries. I shut off my mind to this whole situation to protect myself. Inside, I was hurting so badly that I thought I was going to crack right open under this pressure. I felt betrayed. I was scared. The ride to the grocery store in town was shorter than it should have been. I gave Rory and Stella a curt side-hug and stepped into the white van that said "Mountain Youth Academy" on the side. The door slid closed behind me, shut by one of the Mental Health Associates sent to retrieve me. And that was it. I was locked in.

The drive was about three hours long, and I prayed we'd get into a car accident before making it to the facility. The MHAs, a male driving and a female in the passenger seat in their stupid fake-cheerful yellow polos, kept trying to engage me in conversation. I was too tired and broken to even fake enjoying conversation with them.

I kept my head pressed against the cool glass of the window, welcoming the bumps in the road when my head would bang into the window. I felt like I deserved it. They eventually gave up and resorted to telling me what to expect when I got there. I tuned them out.

Finally, the large brick building loomed in the distance. It looked like a hospital, and I later found it had once been. The MHAs led me through a series of locked doors that could only be opened with a badge or a key. The staff confiscated my suitcase and searched it for contraband, which, until now, had been a foreign word to me. The nurses searched me for any scars, cuts, tattoos, or piercings that they needed to take note of. In case any new ones appeared. They took my bra because it had an underwire in it, and they were afraid I could use it to hurt myself. They took my tennis shoes because of the strings and gave me an ugly, clumpy black pair of Velcro shoes like I was a two-year-old.

Afterward, the MHAs led the group upstairs to the dorms. There were two sides of the building - the boys' dorms were on one side, and the girls' dorms were on the other. The girls' dorms were divided into only two "phases" or sections based on age groups. When I entered Phase II Females from the staff meeting room with doors on either side leading to both sides of the building, the other girls swarmed me like bees swarming a hive.

They all wanted to know my name, what I was "in" for (like this was a prison), and if I *liked* girls. A lot of them, I came to realize, were bi-sexual, though they hadn't identified as such before coming here. I guess it was kind of like a prison in that regard. The girls here ranged from twelve-year-old Emily, who was in because she had been such a bully to her little sister and her classmates. Then there was fifteen-year-old Ariel, who had been in multiple placements like this throughout her lifetime and had no one but her caseworker on her team, as her family had abandoned her. To the left of our dorm, separated by another series of locked doors, was Phase I Females, where the older girls, ages sixteen to almost eighteen, were.

Our MHAs told us to line up for dinner when things settled down. "Phase II Females en route to the cafeteria," was announced on the walkie-talkie. The staff announced our movement to prevent various groups from crossing paths with one another so that the staff could keep up with the schedule. I'd made a few friends already with Melissa, who had the brightest blue eyes and the longest, thickest lashes I'd ever seen on a girl.

She was rail thin because she starved herself, and she had full lips. She could have easily been a model. She had already declared, unabashedly, that she had a crush on me. Another girl, Khadijah, had also made quick friends with me as she would be my roommate.

Her current roommate, Hollisha, would be transported to a different treatment facility the next day. She was currently in the hospital.

I was told, in gory detail, how she had cut her arm at the elbow and shoved objects - pencils, erasers, and pieces of paper - into her arm. Two MHAs transported her to the hospital to have the items removed, and then she was stitched up. When she returned to MYA, she ripped out her stitches and proceeded to repeat the procedure. This time, the girls told me, she was going to be getting a cast to prevent herself from accessing the wound. She was to be returning later in the evening.

Again, I realized I did not fit in. But, for the first time in my life, maybe that wasn't such a bad thing. That night, I had to go to bed by 8:00 PM because I was on the bottom level of this program. There were no empty rooms in Phase I or Phase II Females, and there was one more section of the hallway that was yet to be filled in by patients.

MHAs placed me in the empty dorm because I had no room with the current setup. The room was small, with two twin beds, two dressers, and a bathroom with two feet of door cut off from the top and bottom so the staff could quickly check in on a patient. The windows were frosted over, except for a small six-inch section at the top. I could see the moon peeking in, and I broke down again.

I felt so isolated and lonely. I had a sheet and a thin blanket in the middle of winter, but I wasn't shivering from the cold. I was shaking with fear and brokenness. I finally drifted off to sleep, my worry and anxiety exhausting me.

I awoke in the night to screaming and what sounded like a struggle. I imagined this is what Mom experienced during her many stays in mental hospitals. I was too scared to poke my head into the hallway to see what was happening. I eventually fell back asleep.

The following day, I woke up and joined the Phase II girls in line for breakfast. Hollisha was there, and boy, was she a sight to see. Dark circles rimmed her eyes, and her black hair stuck out in all directions like she'd gotten electrocuted. She looked like your stereotypical insane asylum patient from the horror movies. She introduced herself, showed me her purple cast, and bragged that she would be going to a 23-hour lockdown facility after breakfast. She said she was excited about it.

In Medline, after breakfast, Hollisha had a seizure in the middle of the hallway. Before we were all pushed behind the closest set of double doors, I looked back and saw her flailing on the floor, her cast banging into her face. And so it went: we were directed and observed all day by two staff members in each dorm.

One set of MHAs watched us in the morning and another in the evening. One staff member was assigned to each side of the building at night since there was less activity and less to observe, and the doors separating each dorm were left open. We lined up for breakfast in the morning, depending on which dorm's turn to go first that week.

Our assigned staff members announced our journey to the cafeteria, where lunch ladies served food a la school cafeteria, and we had twenty minutes to eat. Once our time was up, the designated girl for the week wiped down the tables, and we lined up at the door. Our departure was announced on the walkie-talkies, as was our journey to Medline.

Most of the girls were on some kind of mental stability drug - anti-anxiety or anti-depressant of one sort or another. Each girl with a prescription went up to the window one at a time, where they were given their pills in a little condiment cup and a cup of water. They stood there to take their medication in front of the nurses, who then checked the girls' open mouths - under the tongue and in the cheeks - to prevent anyone from deception. Once all the girls had gotten their medication, our staff announced our trip back up to the dorms on the walkie-talkies. When we got upstairs, we were to prepare for morning group therapy with our MHAs.

Each girl had a series of goals to work on for the day based on problems they had or issues they'd talked about with their therapist. We all sat on the wooden-framed couches with the thin cushions in the dayroom and told one of the MHAs which goal we'd be working on that day. They ranged from "I will not curse at inanimate objects" to "I will work on differentiating between rational and irrational thoughts."

Afterward, we had some time to freshen up for the day. I couldn't wear makeup until I earned enough points to work up to my sophomore level. I'd started on orientation, and each day, I was allowed to earn points based on my good behavior. If I caused problems, was disrespectful, or didn't cooperate, I didn't earn my points. I was issued a Negative BCL (Behavior Control Level), which usually results in a punishment chosen by the staff member. They could take things away or put us on a level freeze so we couldn't apply for our levels to level up.

Then, we were taken downstairs for school in the few classrooms they had set up. We had an English class in a room with a small selection of books, and our assignments involved writing about various topics. We had Social Studies, where we worked through multiple modules on some computer programs in the NovaNet computer lab. I didn't read any of it and just guessed my way through it, as did everyone else.

Eventually, we'd use the process of elimination to determine the correct answers enough to pass. Math was with an older lady named Ms. Parker. She gave us worksheets to complete for the week based on our academic performance. On Fridays, she also started painting the girls' nails however we wanted, which helped lift our spirits and self-confidence.

The staff constantly communicated on the radio, and though it drove me crazy to listen to at first, I could quickly block out the constant chatter over the radio. Each patient was assigned a therapist out of the few that worked there, and we were to meet with them one-on-one at least three times a week. Our MHAs had clipboards with observation sheets on us - each had an equal number to divide the workload - and they wrote notes about our interactions with peers and staff members, our cooperation in school, and other daily activities.

We had lunch and time in the rec room when it was cold outside, where we could play foosball and ice hockey, as well as jump rope. In the evenings, we had the freedom to do as we wished - there was a television in the dayroom, and we could read, play board games, do puzzles, play CDs, dance, and play video games. We were on a rotating schedule for evening chores and showers, and once we finished, we had evening group therapy. Each of us took turns discussing whether or not we had completed the goal we'd set out to work on that morning.

Then, the MHAs sent us on the Orientation level to bed. Each level - Freshman, Sophomore, Junior, and Senior - had more privileges and phone time for our weekly call home.

I got one five-minute phone call a week. The only people on my contact list for most of the time I was there were Rory and Stella. I felt trapped in that regard. The phone calls with them were seldom pleasant, as I was still angry with them, and they were still disappointed and distrustful of me. They informed me that Mom had been in Highland, a mental hospital back home, since the end of January as well. The coincidence of that wasn't lost on me. Rory told me that Mom had indicated some bugs in her apartment were reading her thoughts and telling people at work what she was thinking. At this point, Mom hadn't worked in years and had been living on government assistance since she'd been deemed unfit to hold a job.

Additionally, Mom claimed that once she got to Highland and her assigned room, the nurses who were taking her blood were going to ship it off to Paris so the aliens could run tests on it.

From the outside looking in, it's comical because it's so random and far-fetched. But I imagined it from the inside looking out, and it made me sad to think about how scary that must have been for Mom because she believed that. Her schizophrenia had made her so paranoid and delusional that this was her reality.

I was not interested in working at my level. I was not interested in getting better. I was not interested in getting out of there. I was not interested in talking with my therapist, Ms. Sam. I was not interested in facing anything. I was tired of being abandoned by people. I decided to give up.

A few days after my arrival, a new girl, Elizabeth, came, and the focus shifted from me to her. I was finally able to breathe again. Then, they split the two full dorms of girls into three more manageable dorms. I stayed in Phase II, but my roommate got moved to Phase III with the younger girls, and I got a new roommate: Ashlee. I got involved with a girl from what became Phase I Females. Her name was Ebony. She had been "dating" Khadijah - as much as one could "date" there across dorms.

Mostly, that meant passing notes between the doors (or in ceiling tiles in the school bathrooms for the boys) and saying things to each other through the cracks in the doors.

I had never been attracted to girls before, but again, desperate for any cheap imitation of love, I resorted to whatever was available. Ebony was seventeen years old, but she was also very much unhinged. All of us were.

I mean, imagine a group of 8-10 teenage girls whose hormones are all over the place; they each have unresolved trauma, some of them have bipolar, and they're stuck together. Forget *Real Housewives of Wherever.* There should have been a reality television show for Mountain Youth Academy. The drama was constant, and the tensions were almost always high.

Chapter Thirteen: When You Fit Right In

I wasn't any help. I had a short fuse and was incredibly judgmental of the other girls' shortcomings rather than looking at my own. I went off on girls constantly, which usually led to a staff member pulling me away. I never got put into a full restraint like a lot of the other girls did, though, when they were physically attacking someone else. I was also a troublemaker. I used my tote/laundry basket as a bathtub - strategically filling it up using the sink in my bathroom and mixing in shampoo, which they kept locked up. When I wasn't taking tote bubble baths, I was, with wet and soapy legs, using the hallways as a slip n' slide - running and sliding onto my knees in the slippery mess. I once broke a VHS in half in a rage and then used the videotape to tie up a willing MHA for fun. I also enjoyed filling up the enormous 30-gallon trash can in the day room with water, much to the chagrin of the staff members, who had to use absorbing powder - A LOT of absorbing powder - because it was too heavy to move and dump out with the liquid sloshing around everywhere.

That earned me not only a BCL-N, but they also issued the consequence that everything in my room - my bed frame, dresser, clothes, and stuffed moose - was taken away from me. Then, a staff member marched me down to what was known as ISS, but it was just an empty room on the first floor in the back of the building, and we had to spend the whole shift there as punishment. Staff handed out ISS to those of us who had made it clear that we were struggling to cohabitate with our peers, which was me fairly often.

I was a mess, and I was out of control. At the slightest inconvenience, I was punching walls, yelling at someone, cussing someone out, slamming doors, and threatening the other girls. I was hurting so badly that I could barely breathe. As much as I tried to keep it trapped inside so that it reverberated and only affected me, the pain sometimes got so intense that it leaked out in bursts, damaging those around me.

I felt abandoned and unloved. I felt worthless and like I had been a waste of resources. Because I was hurting so badly, I wanted to make others hurt, too. To be fair, each of the girls was hectic in their way. Some were attention seekers, some were criers, and some were violent. I was cruel to the other girls, as was described by Ms. Sam during over-the-phone family sessions, which were once a month with Rory and Stella.

Ms. Sam had access to all the notes on my behaviors during shifts and was aware of my antics. She tried to help me work through the vast steaming pile that had been my life, but I didn't know where to start. My trauma had formed such a tangled mess that had already taken such deep roots. We did talk about some difficult things, don't get me wrong, but it didn't even scratch the surface of everything there was to uncover. I was too scared to peel back the layers of pain.

Ms. Sam went on to informally diagnose me with severe PTSD and Borderline Personality Disorder, neither of which I accepted. She could not formally diagnose me until I was 18 years old and had undergone a series of psychological evaluations. Still, the signs were all there – the unstable relationships, the degrading self-image, the lack of emotional control, which all lead to impulsive behavior.

There was no denying it, yet I refused to acknowledge that I was *that* damaged - there was no way. I'd always thought post-traumatic stress disorder was reserved for veterans and older people - people who were not strong enough to handle the challenges life threw at them. I had survived, though, so I must have been strong enough. I also mistook her suggestion that I had borderline personality disorder with her indicating that I had *Split* Personality Disorder, or Dissociative Personality Disorder (DID) as it's now called.

I knew I had problems, but I also knew I only had one person in my head. Her assessment offended me so much that I shut down and stopped responding to her treatment.

Sometimes, I would make progress and go a week without being "grounded" on BCL-N, but not often, and I would go right back to being a menace. I kept a journal and wrote in it every day to keep track of the days since they all seemed to blur together. There was constant drama, as I'm sure you can imagine, with eight to twelve hormonal teenage girls all grouped together. We weren't allowed pens in our rooms, as that was one of the many items on the long list of contraband, resulting in a level drop if found. They were afraid we'd use the ink for jailhouse-style tattoos. I had to get creative about where I hid my pens so I could write in my journal every night - I didn't want the graphite in the pencil to smear over time and erase my ramblings. I wished to have evidence of my presence and what I'd witnessed. The staff performed room searches regularly, searching inside bathroom doors, under the drawers of our dressers, within our mattresses, and in the frames of our beds. Nothing was off limits. I wasn't doing anything nefarious with my pen, though, and I was able to avoid getting found out.

Writing was a way to help me get all the mess in my head out on paper. It helped me sort through everything by seeing my pain in front of me so I could make sense of it and work through it.

My emotions took up too much room in my head to keep them

there—I often exploded from the pressure. Within the first few months of being there, the staff placed me on "Constant" because the nurse discovered cuts on my thighs where I'd self-harmed with a staple I'd seen in a magazine in one of the classrooms. Constant meant that I had to always be within arms ' length of a staff member who was assigned specifically to me. When I was in the shower, they sat inside the doorway to keep an eye on me while they did their paperwork. When I was using the bathroom, they stood outside my bathroom door to make sure I didn't hurt myself. At night, I had to pull my mattress out into the hallway and sleep right in front of the overnight staff member. Constant was a required three days, but more if I were to show intentions of hurting myself again, which did not happen. I was not a fan of the invasion of privacy. Furthermore, nurses also put students on one-to-one, which meant that they were at serious risk of hurting themselves or others - so severe that they were assigned a staff member in addition to the two MHAs assigned to every dorm. When on one-to-one, the staff member would need to be within arm's length of their patient at all times.

Saturdays were reserved for families to come to visit their loved ones who were patients. There were quite a few Saturdays when everyone in the dorm got to go down for visitations except for me. Stella and Rory said they wouldn't visit me until I started making better choices and showing improvement. I stayed in the dorm alone, save for the staff, often curled into a ball on the couch for hours of visitation time until my dormmates rejoined me.

Ebony and I continued our on-and-off-again "relationship" for months. She would want to be with me, expressing her love for me in her notes. Then, she'd threaten to kill me because of something she'd thought I'd done. I put up with it because I craved that feeling of validation. It was the only way I got any sense of self-worth since I could not produce any independently.

The Mental Health Associates kept the girls as far away from the boys as much as possible, and they prevented our paths from crossing as much as possible, but we did cross paths sometimes. And that's when I laid eyes on Andrew – he had frizzy brown hair and light blue eyes that I fell right into. That's all I knew of him, but I was fifteen and smitten on the spot. I talked one of the new girls in my dorm, Deanna, who was in Psycho-drama with Andrew, into asking if he was interested in me.

She would have to be careful, of course, as Psycho-drama is a serious therapeutic tool that helps kids work through some significant issues in their lives. Staff only granted patients an induction into the program if they were doing well and proved willing to work their program. That was not me.

I could pass notes to him through the classrooms that all the dorms shared and soon found that he was interested in me, too. Pretty much, once I realized that I had dropped Ebony. I was done with the constant roller coaster that was her emotions. I threw myself headfirst into what little relationship I could manage with Andrew. The outdoor play area was on a hill behind the facility, where we often played touch football with some other staff. The boys' side of the building faced the outdoor play area, so Andrew could stand on his window sill and see me through the small section of clear glass at the top of his window. He used to put his hands in the shape of a heart (a la Taylor Swift's *Fearless* Era). I was desperate to hold onto something that gave me hope. His promises that we'd be together when we got out gave me hope, no matter how fickle they were.

Enough hope that, in April, I started to work on my program. It was not at all smooth sailing, as I still had plenty of anger and guilt that I needed to work through.

Ms. Sam indicated she was proud of me when I asked for her signature on my freshman-level application. However, Stella and Rory were still very doubtful, saying that I hadn't changed and was simply fooling everyone. Their lack of faith in me was enough to send me into a tailspin, and, in a rage that evening, I slammed a door in a staff member's face, earning me a level drop.

I no longer had my freshmen level. I lost any progress I'd

made. What was the point in trying if the two people I had to impress wouldn't acknowledge the changes? I was in a dark period, and I frequently wrote about wanting to die in my journal and how I couldn't understand why God had even bothered to spare my life. So many times, He protected me. And for what? So I could suffer and feel this worthless and lonely? I felt like I couldn't do anything right, and I was done trying.

When I earned my freshmen level again after losing it, the staff bumped up my phone time to ten minutes, and I was allowed to stay up thirty minutes later. Some staff members were pretty cool, and I got to know them well. They would listen to me talk and realize when something was amiss. In their wisdom, they explained that I have walls that inhibit me from letting people get too close.

Anytime someone did anything that made me feel betrayed or felt the threat of being abandoned, I pushed them away before I could get hurt. Once they brought that to my attention, I became more aware of how I treated the other girls. Many of these girls saw me as a leader, and just like I'd let down Harper, Sadie, and Amelia, I was also letting them down by being so cruel to them.

Rory and Stella visited me in April, and things were tense. I kept expressing my disinterest in going back to live with them. I was willing to go anywhere else - foster home, group home, be emancipated- anything to get away from them. Stella indicated that I was not mature or responsible enough to live independently. I vehemently disagreed, of course, at fifteen years old because I thought I knew everything. And I thought that I would be able to get out of there, run off with Andrew into the sunset, and live happily ever after. My naivety was sickening. I'd seen a few too many Disney princess movies and had developed unrealistic expectations for love. I saw Andrew as my prince charming and savior – who would magically make everything okay.

Andrew had been working his program, doing all the right things to get out of Mountain Youth Academy as quickly as possible. He could fake it until he made it, and he was good at it. In Psychodrama, participants were able to work through their trauma by acting it out. He flew through his levels, and by August, he was ready to graduate.

I was only on my sophomore level - it had been a roller coaster of a journey to get there. I'd gotten level drops for outbursts and hugging a friend. I'd worked hard for my levels and was proud of my progress. While I had made progress as it pertained to coping with my negative emotions, I hadn't started to uproot those negative emotions and find out what caused them.

Ms. Sam prescribed me antidepressants, which acted as another bandage for the trauma and hurt. My sophomore level had more privileges: I could wear makeup and jewelry to make myself feel pretty again. I could stay up until 9 PM, so my friend Sara - also on her sophomore level - and I stayed up and watched scary movies that the staff had rented. I channeled my anger into something more productive and created more fun chaos in my world instead of a violent one. That summer, per my request, we had bonfires where we roasted s'mores, had a proper slip n' slide outside, and played football. I was desperately trying to distract myself from what was coming. I remember thinking constantly about how I wished life was like a book - I had always been an avid reader - and I could skip to the end to see how things would turn out before I continued. I had to make sure what was to come would be worth it before I chose to continue.

When Andrew left at the end of August, I watched him walk out to his social worker's grey car from the little section at the top of the window in my room that I could see through. Kids constantly came to and went from Mountain Youth Academy, but his leaving wrecked me. People I cared about had proven time and time again throughout my life that I couldn't trust them to stay, nor could I trust them to uphold their promises and not betray me.

Stella broke the news during one of our phone calls that month that she was eight months pregnant. Her oncologist had cleared her to start trying for kids again sometime in the previous year, and she hadn't wasted any time. Spencer was seven years old, so Rory and Stella had much catching up to do. She claimed they didn't tell me because they wanted me to work on my program, and her disclosing the information when she did was my reward for good behavior.

Stella visited me in August, and I was surprised to see how swollen and rounded her belly was. I'd been too young to understand or care the last time either of my sisters was pregnant, so I paid more attention this time. She was able to call me on the day she gave birth to break the news to me. I broke down crying in the phone call closet. I was happy for her and the fact that she had welcomed a new life.

At the same time, my insecurities dug their claws into me, and I worried the latest addition would replace me in Stella's heart. I also feared that everyone's life was moving on and getting better outside the walls and barbed wire fences of Mountain Youth Academy, and I was stuck there.

So stuck that I spent my 16th birthday behind the confines of what was a mental hospital for teenagers. I'd grown up watching *My Sweet Sixteen* on MTV, so the idea that a girl's 16th birthday was a big deal and a rite of passage was deeply ingrained in who I was.

I knew I would never be able to have a massive party like those girls from the show in any version of my reality, both in and out of Mountain Youth Academy. But I was still incredibly disappointed, despite the pink cupcakes and birthday cards I received from my dorm mates. I saw my sweet sixteenth birthday end with my face buried in my pillow - to dampen the noise - while I sobbed at the pathetic state of my life. And again, I begged for death to welcome me. I was so tired of fighting against myself every day. I'd never learned how to live, and I still hadn't figured it out.

We were all still trying to figure out where I would go after Mountain Youth Academy - Stella, Rory, my new therapist - Ms. Sarah - and myself. I was still adamant that I didn't want to return to Rory and Stella's. I knew I'd messed up.

I didn't want to go back with them and face their looks of disappointment. I also felt betrayed and abandoned by them, just like I had been by everyone else. I was done relying on people to take care of me - I had learned to rely solely on myself because I was the one person I could trust.

This ideology was reinforced even more in October when I got a letter from a friend who had left MYA just a few months prior. Our therapists always opened and inspected our mail before they gave it to us.

So, when a look of pity crossed Ms. Sarah's face as she handed me my letter from Deanna, I felt dread in the pit of my stomach. Deanna had graduated from and left Mountain Youth Academy just a few months prior, and after begging Rory and Stella to put her on my contact list, they finally did. I unfolded the letter, recognizing Deanna's fat and preppy handwriting immediately. My eyes frantically scanned the letter, searching for the bad news that I was sure to come. And then I found it: "Andrew is with another girl." Bile rose in my throat, and my world closed in around me. My ears started ringing; Ms. Sarah's muffled voice called out to me, and it sounded like she was underwater. I wasn't going to let myself fall apart here. I reeled it in, sat up straight, and declared I was okay. He was just a stupid boy, right?

Tears blurred my vision, and my throat threatened to close up as I choked back tears during my half-hour therapeutic phone call with Rory and Stella. Afterward, I asked if I could return to the dorm, and Ms. Sarah hesitated before agreeing. She looked at me like a wild animal that could attack any minute. As soon as I crossed the threshold of my room, I lost my composure.

I fell to my knees and sobbed deeply from within my chest. I'd put all of my faith in Andrew and our future together. He only lived an hour and a half from where I'd grown up; we'd made plans for a future together after we left all this behind.

I felt like my heart was cracking in half - the two halves pulling away from each other in agony. I ran to the bathroom and heaved, gagged, and puked up what little contents were in my stomach. One of my favorite staff members was working our dorm that evening, and she came in and rubbed my back until I crumbled to the floor in a shaking, clammy mess. She quietly informed me that the boys and the girls were switching sides of the building, and I needed to pack my stuff and move as if my life was not chaotic enough.

Then, I heard the sounds of movement and shuffling in the hallway. It's not like we had much to move - just our personal belongings, which didn't amount to much.

In a trance, I packed up my clothes, journals, stuffed animals, and blankets in my tote and carried them across the hallway to the other side of the building - where Andrew had spent the whole of his seven-month stay.

The insecurities washed over me like a tsunami - why was I never good enough? Why wasn't I enough to make anyone want to stay? Why was someone always chosen over me? Over the following days, I reverted to the old Destinee - I became combative and argumentative. I lashed out at staff members and my dorm mates.

I started making myself throw up after every meal, thinking that maybe if I lost a little weight, I'd be worthy of someone's love and affection. I was on the verge of getting a level drop after I'd already earned my junior level. I was now eligible for a home pass that allowed me to spend my first twenty-four hours at home since arriving here just to test the waters and see how things would go. Juniors were often then granted a forty-eight-hour home pass a few weeks later. I had already earned and scheduled my home pass and was just a few weeks away. Losing my junior level over some boy would be detrimental to my progress and Rory and Stella's already fragile belief in me.

One of the staff members with whom I was incredibly close finally pulled me aside and talked some sense into me. I stopped feeling sorry for myself and instead just bottled it up inside since my negative emotions were making everyone around me uncomfortable. I got into Psychodrama, and Ms. Sarah said the reason she didn't let me in before was because of my behavior, but I knew it was also because of Andrew. By this point, though, it was too late - I'd already shut down to being helped. I just numbed myself to everything to protect myself. I went on my home pass and got to meet and hold Shiloh. It took me back to when I held his older brother, Spencer, for the first time. Things went well, and I gave up trying to live elsewhere. It was apparent that nobody else wanted me. I had to face what I'd done and the mess I'd made.

I continued to work my way up the totem pole of success as defined by the fine folk at Mountain Youth Academy. I'd finally earned my senior level and was on my way to applying for my official "Program Completion." I had enough points, and I'd already filled out the paperwork; I just needed a couple more signatures, but many administrators were out of the building because of the holiday season.

On Christmas morning, each dorm got to go down to the meeting room where we had our Psycho Drama meetings and eat cookies, drink hot chocolate, and open our stockings and presents. Each student got presents sent from home, and the staff chipped in to buy us each a present. I got to stay after all the girls from my dorm left and opened the rest of my gifts. Mom had sent so many presents - to make up for her lack of presence in my life - that the staff didn't want the other girls to feel jealous. It was nice to have so many presents, but I still felt so alone.

We woke up on New Year's Day to a present from one of the head administrators of the entire building: he had granted everyone their next level - if they had the points - without the need to apply. The supervisor awarded me my Program Completion. In any other circumstance, I would have been stoked to have gotten this far, considering where I started.

But the sense of accomplishment was ripped away because I hadn't *earned* it. I hadn't gotten my application in with the last few signatures, though it wouldn't have been more than a week or two before I had. I felt cheated.

The last few weeks I was there, I was busy getting my goodbye book signed, a widespread tradition among graduates or people who knew they'd be leaving soon, even if they didn't complete their program. Students passed around a notebook or composition book and had the other girls in the dorm sign it and their favorite staff members.

Mine was full of endearing notes from staff members calling me "Spunky Monkey" and "Bubbles" because of my bubbly personality. I had grown to be passionate about anything and everything - just like my mom before me - even when I was mad at the world.

On my last night, before I headed back to West Virginia for good, it was getting pretty late, and I still hadn't had a goodbye party like I'd helped put together for all the other girls. It hurt my heart.

I mentioned it to the evening supervisor, whom I'd view as a father figure as he often played football with us in the evenings. He looked upset, and then I was sent down to the Rec Room, where I'd learned to double-Dutch with another group of girls.

We played and had fun while the evening supervisor sent our recreation teacher on a mission to help plan a surprise goodbye party for me. The evening supervisor commented that if anyone deserved a goodbye party, it was me.

I came upstairs to the dayroom, which my dormmates had decked out with balloons and banners just for me. I tossed and turned that night, my mind refusing to sort through every possible outcome of my return home. I didn't know what to expect.

On the way home in February 2010, Danny Gokey's "My Best Days Are Ahead of Me" came on the radio, and I took that as a sign that

God was telling me it would be all right.

Chapter Fourteen: Things Will Never Be the Same

I got home, and Stella and I talked for a long time. I apologized for what I'd put them through and promised to do better. She dropped the bomb on me that she was pregnant again and would have this baby - also a boy - only thirteen months after her last one. She also explained that Spencer was now in my old room with all my old furniture - the lovely, real-wood furniture they'd purchased just for me. Shiloh had taken Spencer's old room, which meant there were no more rooms in the house. I would, therefore, be sleeping on the couch upstairs. *Lovely*, I thought. Out of all the kids in the house now, I was the oldest and in the greatest need of a room for privacy. I kept my mouth shut, though, to keep the peace. I was glad to be somewhere without the constant drama and to have more peace.

She told me she still loved me, but because of what we'd been through, her feelings toward me had changed and were no longer the same. My heart sank because I should have known. I needed love more than anything, and I couldn't earn it anywhere. I was determined to try to earn their favor. She could not love me as a parent unconditionally loves their children because I was not her child, nor would I ever be.

She also reminded me that George Washington High School refused to accept me back since I was out of district anyway - as if I could have forgotten. Instead, I would be going to Herbert Hoover High School and returning to the kids I grew up with after two years away. It wouldn't be that bad, right?

I still used a little battery-powered MP3 player at Mountain Youth Academy. I'd used music to help me drown out all the noise and drama around me and replace it with more pleasant sounds. Rory and Stella had also issued me a government-funded trac phone since I had a medical card. So, there I was - generations of technology behind my classmates – once again trying to fit in and not draw attention to myself.

The questions and rumors were instantaneous: "I heard you ran away and got pregnant. Is that true?" "Where have you been?" "I'm glad you're not on drugs anymore." "Why were you having sex with random guys in the hallways at school?" And on and on and on.

The bullying took a while to build up, but once the shock of my return wore off, it was almost unbearable. Boys would yell stuff out to me in the stairwell about my suspension. I should have known that everyone would have found out. Technology, social media, and communication were getting to the point that almost everyone had access to them, and news traveled fast now.

By the end of the first month, I was begging Stella to pull me out and homeschool me. I couldn't take the bullying anymore. I couldn't stand the classes that were absolute wastes of time: my biology teacher loved blowing up powder-filled latex gloves, my health teacher showed us random movies, and my Geometry teacher gave us packets every week that I got credit for even though I only scribbled in them. I enjoyed my English class and found opportunities to heal a bit through some of the writing I did while I was there. Otherwise, I was miserable but stuck it out because I felt I deserved it. I felt like this was God's way of punishing me for the mess I'd made of my life.

Being homeschooled was the only way I could get away from the constant barrage of insults and slurs. I kept my head down as I sulked through the hallways that seemed to get narrower daily. I pretended to busy myself by typing furiously on my TracPhone to mimic texting. I must have looked ridiculous, especially because iPhones were already mainstream.

I was so incredibly and lamely behind the times. My mp3 player ran on AA batteries that I kept drained of juice; nevertheless, I kept my headphones in my ears to give the impression that I couldn't hear the insults they spat at me. I was too beaten down and cowardly to stand up for myself. Subconsciously, I believed I deserved all of this. I felt I was so undeserving of love that I let it happen.

Despite the thirteen months of in-patient therapy, my perception of myself hadn't changed at all. I'd learned to disassociate so much from my pain that I wasn't able to identify with it or work through it. I just got good at hiding it. I still hated myself, felt unloved, and believed I was unworthy of love. Even with Rory and Stella, life was easier because I had gotten myself - my behaviors - more under control because I'd caved in on myself and turned more inward. I felt tolerated more than anything.

I finally convinced Stella to homeschool me for my junior year of high school, even though I knew that I would be giving up. This time was over a decade before COVID-19 hit, and everyone became too anti-social and awkward for social gatherings, back when homecoming games and dances, prom, and graduation were everything. I was willing to give it up without hesitation because I was so miserable and embarrassed.

I felt like Hester Prynne, wearing her shame on her bosom for the world to see and judge and sneer at. I counted down the days until my sentence was up. I got through the second semester of my tenth-grade year with an easy 4.0 GPA, much to the dismay of my peers.

I started homeschooling a couple of weeks after the end of the public school year. The curriculum Stella chose was Christian-based and very advanced compared to what I was used to. I've always been eager to learn, so she knew I would adapt well. I struggled at first. I went from having four pathetic excuses for classes to having eight advanced courses. Had I had the foundation that students usually build going through years of this program, I would have been on top of my game. I had not had that foundation, nor anything close. I was learning about diagramming sentences, which I had never even heard of - math and English mixing. What in the world? I took a Family Consumer Science class, which was much more than just learning to cook. I learned about table etiquette, which would have been helpful when staying with my friend Eleanor and her family. I learned how to set a complete table with all the spoons, forks, and extra dishes like I'd seen on *Titanic*. I planned a rolled cake tea party for which I invited Mom over and served my made-from-scratch strawberry rolled cake.

They had a room built onto their house in the extra living room space in the basement. A few months later, we picked up a dresser and an armoire at a yard sale. They'd given my real-wood furniture to their kids in my absence. On the bright side, I finally had my own room, was homeschooled, and wasn't getting bullied. I loved watching Stella's belly grow and Shiloh grow and learn, and I was getting outside in the sunshine every day - walking up and down the steep hill we lived on. Then, I started making stupid mistakes because I was trying hard to be perfect. I worried that if I wasn't perfect, I'd get sent away again, or they'd give up on me, and I wouldn't have anyone. I was afraid to ask questions and couldn't handle being criticized or judged for asking stupid questions.

I had to make a steak dinner for one of my assignments. The recipe called for 12 ounces of meat, and we had gone to the store and got a package of beef just for the assignment. The meat, however, was marked to be 12.8 ounces or something. So, in my head, it made sense if I wanted the recipe to turn out perfectly, to cut off the excess. I pulled the little kitchen scale out of the drawer and cut pieces off of the hunk of meat until there were precisely 12 ounces left. What I cut off, I just discarded. We didn't have a dog or anything to give the scraps to, so it made sense. There wasn't enough to salvage and do anything with.

Since this meal was the first I would be cooking for them entirely alone, I felt immense pressure for it to be impeccable. After the meal, when we cleaned up, everyone complimented how good everything tasted. I beamed and then bragged that I even made a point to trim away the extra meat so that the seasoning proportions and everything would be perfect. I was so proud of myself for going the extra mile. They were not happy that I had wasted so much meat. Stella yelled at me, which was nothing new, and asked me how I could be so stupid, often followed by: Where is your common sense? I hung my head in shame and sulked to my room. Another assignment required me to make bread from scratch, which can be lengthy, depending on the bread you choose. I don't remember what kind it was; it only required a lot of flour and a lot of kneading. The flour was messy, but I did my best to clean it up before heading outside to play with Spencer and Shiloh.

When I returned inside, Stella yelled at me again, claiming she had gotten on her hands and knees at eight months pregnant to clean up the flour I had left on the floor. Her tone and word choice showed she thought I'd intentionally left the mess out of laziness or irresponsibility. I tried to explain to both her and Rory that was not the case - the color of the laminate kitchen floor made it difficult to see any flour that I may have left.

I felt like I couldn't do anything right. No wonder nobody seemed to want me or truly love me. I did my best to help out around the house and win the favor of Rory and Stella. As her due date neared, I did my best to improve my game. I watched, changed, bathed, and fed Shiloh whenever I could. I enjoyed the connection and the feeling of him falling asleep on me. He depended on me and admired me for caring for him, and I loved it. I stayed behind when she went to the hospital to help Rory's mom clean the house for the new baby's return.

When Stella was ready to give birth, she let me back in the room with her during the delivery. The atmosphere was intense; everyone was on the edge of their seats, waiting for this baby to be born. When it was finally time for her to push, I stood at the end of the bed, out of the way as much as I could. As the baby boy burst into this world, my heart filled with amazement and wonder.

Rory handed me the oversized pair of surgical steel scissors afterward and suggested I cut the cord. With shaking hands, I sliced through the life link between mother and child, and it felt like I was cutting through lunch meat. As gross as that sounds, it was the most magical thing I'd ever seen – a precious life brought into this world and a testament to God's creation. It was then that I decided that I wanted to become a midwife. I set my heart on delivering babies and watching women turn into mothers.

I'd reconnected through Facebook with my old friend from my foster care, Chelsea. She was still the same ole dimpled red-headed beauty I barely remembered. Trauma will do that to you, I've learned. It makes you remember the bad times vividly as a warning system for your psyche so that you can store it away as a warning of what to expect in the future. It's a defense mechanism, so you aren't surprised.

We picked up as if nothing had changed - we started talking on the phone frequently, and I could reconnect with Tammy and Kevin through her. Kevin would bring my former foster brother, Cody, and

Chelsea with him when he came to pick me up. They all would have been in camouflage and out hunting all morning. Chelsea seemed so sure of herself, well put together, and mature that I was envious of her. She was the cool kid, and I was not. She was beautiful, and I was not. She wore her naturally curly hair, which looked stunning, but my natural curls looked unruly.

Also, through Facebook, I reconnected with Andrew from Mountain Youth Academy, and based on his profile pictures, being on the outside had done him well. I was instantly smitten all over again. You'd think I would have learned my lesson the first time, but I was still hungry and desperate for more.

He and I talked on and off for years. Pain is an adhesive, and he and I had connected during and through our trauma, which is what bonded us together in ways we'd never bond with anyone else. He was an hour and a half away, but I didn't want to get involved in anything that would jeopardize Rory and Stella's trust in me even more than I already had. Most of the time, I did a pretty good job.

Ms. Sarah and I had thought we'd located Brandon in North Carolina while I was at Mountain Youth Academy. I had just assumed at that point that I would never get to meet him. So, when Stella came up the stairs one evening while I was relaxing on the couch and told me that she'd found Brandon on Facebook, my heart sank to my stomach. I was seventeen years old at the time and had honestly kind of given up on the idea of ever meeting him. I was content without meeting him, and I worried that meeting him would disrupt my life's lack of chaos. I didn't know whether to be happy, sad, excited, or anxious. She also told me that she'd found my sister, Hannah, and that she and Brandon lived in the surrounding areas.

Stella and Rory helped me draft a Facebook message to Hannah. I wasn't sure if she knew I existed or if I'd just been some dirty little secret. I wasn't sure how she'd react to learning about me or hearing from me.

Once we finally drafted a message wherein I introduced myself and indicated my desire to meet, I hit send and anxiously awaited her reply. I wanted to meet her first before I met Brandon.

She messaged me back not even a day later, indicating that she had known about me. She also lamented that Brandon had not been a father to her, either, as he tended to be in and out of her life. She also started making excuses for him, indicating that he was socially awkward, which could be why he didn't contact me. We messaged back and forth before agreeing to meet at the mall food court.

We both got Japanese cuisine, and we chatted. It was easy, and everyone got along great. I found out Hannah had gone to college and gotten a degree, that she loved video games and anime, and that she loved cats. I mostly saw video games as a waste of time, believed cartoons were for adults, and was allergic to cats. We didn't have anything in common at all.

We ended the evening with many hugs and promises to keep in touch. We found it challenging to forge a relationship that's meant to be built on a life-long connection.

Hannah and I went out together a few times - always things she wanted to do, like going out for sushi or going to weird stores selling incense - while her husband drove us around. Hannah always wore long sleeves, no matter the heat or humidity.

She explained to me that she, too, had psoriasis, but it was all over her chest, arms, and legs, whereas mine was only on the back of my head. She said it ran on Brandon's side of the family, so the psoriasis was yet another aspect about myself that I'd gotten from Brandon and that I hated.

Now that I'd gotten to know his other daughter and could understand what he'd been like with her, Brandon was less intimidating. I reached out to him like I had Hannah, but I knew he knew about me. There was no denying it. In his profile picture, he was potbellied with a gray mustache, his right hand on the steering wheel of his boat, and a beer can on his left.

He looked much worse for the wear than he did in the pictures that Mom had given me. In those, he had dark brown hair and a relatively slim figure despite some prominent love handles. I tried to imagine what he'd be like and what it would be like to meet him finally.

Every scenario possible ran through my mind in the weeks leading up to our meeting. I tried not to get my hopes up because I wasn't holding my breath for a normal father-daughter relationship. He'd had seventeen years to establish one at that point. And yet, I was the one who was stuck reaching out.

Stella refused to go with me because she knew she couldn't control herself and her anger around him. After all, he abandoned me. Instead, Rory went with me, as did Hannah, whom Wyatt dropped off. Brandon looked just like he did in his Facebook picture. His belly stuck out from him, and he smelled like a cigarette. We took awkward photos against the wall by our table at the restaurant.

He insisted that he looked for me, which Hannah backed up. They looked for me when they moved to North Carolina and New York, as if, for some reason, that's where I would be. I never went anywhere, not really, and my name never changed. He could have located me had he wanted to.

After he dealt out what I'm sure he felt were the mandatory apologies, Brandon bragged about how big his television was, all gaming consoles, his favorite video games, and his boat.

Meanwhile, he's gotten off scot-free when it came to me. It was like I never existed. I was his bastard child that he never had to take responsibility for.

He promised to be a better father now that he'd "found" me, even though I was the one who had reached out to him. He offered to take me out on his boat, and it felt like a slap to the face.

After eating and checking out at the front, Brandon paid for his meal and stepped to the side. Rory and I were baffled. Rory paid for my meal without hesitation, and Brandon and I exchanged numbers as we walked to his light blue pickup truck.

I was the one who reached out and called him, and I kept it up for a few weeks until I realized that he was not interested. I wouldn't waste my energy contacting him if he didn't reciprocate my efforts. I'm not going to lie; it hurt, but the wound was already gaping and putrid as it was. It was nothing I couldn't handle.

At one point, Brandon messaged me, berating me for allowing my "want to be dad," Rory, to prevent father and daughter from connecting. Nobody was in the way. Brandon needed to put in some effort and reach out - show his maturity and acceptance of responsibility by forming a bond. But instead, he chose to forego any reaching out.

It was a hard pill to swallow and one that I wouldn't be able to digest for years to come. I was frustrated that Brandon still had everyone fooled. Here he was, living his life as this well-respected man in society, and I was mentally and emotionally damaged and suffering seemingly beyond repair. Life is so unfair.

I went to the dentist again that fall, and they told me that I needed to get my wisdom teeth taken out immediately. The dentist told me he had never seen a seventeen-year-old with roots on their wisdom teeth as long as mine. They were so long that they were on the verge of digging into my jawbone or cutting into the nerve that runs along where the jawbone and gums meet. Either way, the dentist told me that if my teeth were allowed to grow much longer, the roots could cause permanent damage to my jawbone or make the extraction risky for the integrity of my nerves. When I had the surgery done only a few days before Thanksgiving, I was terrified of being put under. I had never had an IV, and I was frightened and grossed out at needles going into my skin.

Afterward, I woke up wholly dazed and with my cheeks swollen and bruised. I lost about twenty pounds within the first few days because I was in so much pain and such a fog from the prescription pain medication.

The surgery restricted my diet to only mashed potatoes and pumpkin pie on Thanksgiving when we went to one of Rory's many family members – not that I was complaining, as those are two of my favorite foods.

I slathered on makeup to cover up the bruising so that I didn't look like a victim of domestic violence. On one of the last pretty days of that fall, I accompanied Stella and the boys to the park to help corral them before the weather changed for the winter season. While there, I picked up a stomach bug because my immune system was not firing on all cylinders as usual. That night, I woke up shivering and unable to warm up despite sleeping in my coat bundled under the blankets. I spent the first hour that I was awake throwing up violently and loudly, much to the dismay of Rory, who was quietly trying to get out the door for work. He checked on me quickly before he left for the day. After Stella got up, she told me to clean the downstairs bathroom I had been puking in. When I told her that I felt weak from being sick, as well as from the pain meds and my surgery, she told me that she cleaned her toilet when she was ill from her cancer radiation treatment, so I would be okay to clean up the bathroom on my own. I forced myself to muster up the strength to clean it since I didn't want Stella to be mad at me.

Chapter Fifteen: Don't Lose Yourself

Homeschooling had been beneficial in helping me learn. The program I was using was big on repetition, which helped me retain the new knowledge the teachers threw at me during every lesson. That and the fact that I had a natural gift for remembering details – it had been a survival tactic for me all these years – I was naturally a good test-taker. Stella and Rory pushed me into college and helped me prepare as much as possible. They believed that education would be my only hope, as that is what Stella claimed saved her. I took the ACT in the spring of my junior year of high school in the middle of my Algebra 2 course. I checked out thick practice test books from the local library and studied and practiced as much as I could before the test.

I felt the weight of my future that rode on the results of this test. I felt the weight of Stella and Rory's expectations for the results of this test. I walked into one of the local high schools with some of the same kids I'd gone to public school with.

Rather than acknowledge them, I pretended I didn't know who they were as I slid into my plastic desk awkwardly. I didn't know how they expected us to be able to concentrate on "one of the most important tests of our lives" with our tailbones digging into hard plastic. Nevertheless, I clasped my newly sharpened number two pencil as the sheets of paper containing the problems and questions I would need to decipher for almost three hours were slid face down onto my desk by the instructor. My heart pounded in my chest at the thought that I could mess this up and render myself a loser in society before I even had the chance to get started.

I was familiar with most of the material, except for the math's last bit. I anxiously awaited my results to be announced via email. Much to my chagrin, I had earned the necessary scores for each subject to get one of the most highly sought-after scholarships in West Virginia. My confidence skyrocketed.

I was getting along pretty well, or so I seemed to be. I'd buried everything and was putting all of my energy and focus into trying to be who Rory and Stella wanted me to be. I was just trying my best to impress them and make them proud.

I was like a dog; I was rewarded, happy, and bubbly whenever I was a good girl. But whenever I was terrible and reprimanded, I tucked my tail and ran, unwilling to face the disappointment in their eyes.

We also fought the way typical sisters fight, which made the relationship even more difficult than it already was. We were both petty. On one occasion, Stella was mad at me for something I can't remember now. Rather than talk to each other, we just stayed away from each other. I stayed in my room with the door closed and did my schoolwork. When dinner time came, I didn't want to join them. When Stella asked me if I was coming up for dinner, I lied and told her I wasn't hungry. In reality, I didn't want to be around her. We fed off each other's negativity and were both petty in our treatment of each other, as sisters typically are.

Nothing about my life so far had ever been easy, and being parented by a sibling was not easy, nor had it ever been. Because of my pride, I stayed in my room and ate bits of a Halloween-themed faux-gingerbread house I had made at the local library a few days before. I couldn't eat the whole thing, as the librarian who helped us said that the graham crackers were old, and she used either super glue or a hot glue gun to secure the crackers into the shape of a haunted house. My growling stomach eventually lulled me to sleep that night. We didn't address it the next day and went along like nothing had happened.

Stella and I loved watching *ABC's 2020* together on Friday evenings – Rory would run out to McDonald's and grab us a midnight snack. We would also stay up watching movies that we couldn't watch with the kids or Stella and I would laugh until tears ran down our cheeks and we couldn't catch our breath.

Meanwhile, I was making new friends in my homeschool group. We went to the local YMCA once a week and played various sports in 6-week increments for our "gym credit" and socialization. First was flag football, then volleyball and basketball. We also went to the ice-skating rink once a month to hang out and get to know each other. I eventually got pretty good at ice skating and gained a good amount of speed and stability.

Ever the one to fall in and out of love easily, I quickly developed a crush on one of the blue-eyed boys in the homeschool group – I'd always had a thing for blue-eyed boys. And I was trying to distract myself from the other blue-eyed boy still tugging at my heartstrings. But I did something different. Rather than allow myself to fall head over heels, I wanted to take my time.

Karter and I developed a friendship quickly. We messaged back and forth through Facebook nearly every day. We talked about anything and everything. We spoke on the phone pretty often in the evenings, too.

I would listen to him while he worked on his car, country music playing in the background. We ice skated together and sat next to each other when a group of the homeschooled kids decided they wanted to see the new *Harry Potter* movie in theaters. But for the first time, I wasn't chasing him. I wasn't desperately begging for attention from him or anything. He came from a lovely Christian family, and his siblings' names also began with the letter K. He came over, and we watched *Pearl Harbor* together.

Stella and Rory kept the kids downstairs so we could have some privacy. Afterward, I walked him out to his Jeep, and he showed off his newly installed stereo system. He had driven to my house, but Rory and Stella wouldn't let me ride as a passenger with him anywhere because they knew what teenage boys were like.

As fall faded into winter, the high school-aged students were gearing up for the local homeschool social. It was like the public school version of prom, only much classier and sophisticated. I was excited to participate in the ritual of dressing up in a fancy dress and getting the experience. Apart from her wedding, prom is a girl's biggest day. I was putting all my cards in one basket as I eagerly waited for Karter to ask me to be his date. And I waited, and I waited. I tried my best to stay positive, keep a level head, and wait for things to fall into place.

Then, one day in early spring, I stayed at the YMCA long past the high school-aged homeschool gym class had ended. I had an interview with one of the local hospitals to volunteer that summer to get experience for when I went to college for midwifery.

I showered and got ready for my interview, and Karter was friendly enough to drive to Wendy's and bring me back some spicy nuggets.

When I asked him who he was taking to the spring formal, I was surprised to hear him say the name of another girl in our homeschool group. I was hoping that he would say no one, I would say no one, and then it would lead to this beautiful moment when he asked me to be his date. I didn't expect this. I was so surprised that I almost choked on the spicy nugget I had popped into my mouth to keep myself occupied so my nerves didn't make me combust. I felt so betrayed. I felt like he'd slapped me. I had never seen him even interact with this girl. Immediately, I started on my spiral: what did this girl have that I didn't, what was so good about this girl that I was lacking, why did he choose her over me, why was I never enough? And even though I had tried to befriend this girl, I found myself hating her, blaming her for stealing a man who wasn't mine to claim.

The girl's dad was a pastor, which gave her serious brownie points over me. Some of the bones in one of her feet hadn't grown correctly, which affected her walking and inhibited her from participating in sports activities. I hyper-focused on that flaw and all the ways that I outshone that specific flaw to make me feel better about myself. I told you I hadn't changed. Not really.

All the work the world saw I'd done was surface level. I still hadn't dug down into the roots of everything. I'd simply put a bandage on all of the gashes that had been my wounds, taken some medication, and called it a day. The infection was still under the surface, waiting for the right time to strike. I'm surprised how long it laid dormant.

Karter came over one evening randomly, stating that he was in the area. We lived on top of a considerable hill way back on a mountain, and he lived in the rich part of town. No one he knew lived out my way except me and the preacher's daughter he was taking to the dance. She lived at the bottom of our hill and just down the road. He claimed he had come out too early to see his girl and needed somewhere to hang out to pass the time. He was dressed nicely in a button-up shirt, brand-new jeans, and cowboy boots, probably to meet her family for the first time.

First impressions were important, and he had a big impression to make on the preacher. I was impressed, and I wish he'd gone to such great lengths to make a good first impression on my folks. Still, as hopeful and as desperate as ever to be loved, I felt so special that he thought to come to me. It never occurred to me that he was simply using me.

I noticed his tag stuck to the thigh of his pant leg while we were lazily swinging on the playground in the backyard and pointed it out to him. He ripped it off and thanked me for saving him the embarrassment of meeting a pastor with a tag still on his pants. I was being friend-

zoned hard, and I didn't even realize it. I'd never been friend-zoned

before. I was not used to guys turning me down. It wasn't because I was

overly attractive or anything like that; it simply was because I was easy

and desperate, and when guys needed an ego boost, I was their

girl. That's how it had been all through middle and high school before I

got suspended.

After he had killed enough time before his important date, off he

went.

"Karter still had a tag stuck on his pant leg," I chuckled to Rory as

I climbed the external stairs of their mid-entry home.

"Yeah, I saw it, too. I just didn't say anything because he came to

hang out with you before he went to see the girl he chose over you." He

smiled.

"I didn't want him to embarrass himself," I said innocently.

"That was the whole point," Rory replied, and I couldn't help but

laugh and feel contentment at how he showed me that he had my back.

Before things petered out between us completely, Karter

suggested I go to the social with his best friend, whom I'd never met, as

he was not athletic either and never went to the gym sessions.

Wanting to not appear like a loser for my first experience going

to a prom-like event, I agreed. I picked out my dress from a second-hand store, which I was okay with. I'd been raised on bargains and thrifting, so it didn't bother me a bit. I met Karter's friend at the local Kohl's to pick out a tie to match the shade of the satin fabric of my dress. He was lanky and awkward and not at all what I was interested in or what had drawn me to Karter. But I didn't want to hurt his feelings like Karter had hurt me, so I went along with it.

When the day finally came, Stella curled my long, untamable brown curly hair for me, she painted my nails that I'd allowed to grow out, and I got my make-up professionally done at Clinique.

I felt beautiful for the first time and was heartbroken that Karter didn't see me this way. I was also heartbroken because I knew that it was supposed to be my mom getting me ready for this moment, but it, like so many other moments in my life, had been thrown completely off course by her choices and actions. Still, I kept my head up and smiled for Rory as he captured pictures of me in my get-up, trying my best to be convincing.

The social was at a local country club, which was fancy even by poor West Virginia standards. The expanse of property boasted courtyards, small garden areas, and golf courses for the well-off in and around the area.

Unlike today's proms, our social event offered a multi-course meal the staff served to us on fancy glass dishes. We were all seated at beautifully decorated and set tables, and I barely spoke to Stephen the entire time. Meanwhile, I tried my best to avoid looking for, or at, Karter and his date as much as possible because I knew that green monster of jealousy would rear her little head, and I would start critiquing things about her. I busied myself by dancing with the few friends I'd made and talking with one of the other girls in the group, who was incredibly socially awkward and considered an outcast in the group. She was a little odd and could have had some kind of autism, but she was always really nice to me, so I made a point to be nice to her in return.

By the end of it, I'd had a great time. I mainly had taken on the role of a tomboy who wore basketball shirts and t-shirts and just pulled my unruly hair into a ponytail. So when the other girls saw me dressed nicely with my hair and make-up done, they were surprised and went on and on about how beautiful they thought I looked and how green my eyes were, especially in contrast to the red of my dress.

When the night ended, I felt like Cinderella after the clock struck midnight. I felt like my night of magic was over, and I was back to being the ugly pumpkin that nobody even bothered to notice. I tried blending into the background and reminding myself I was not exceptional.

That summer was a busy one for me. I started my senior year – yes, I started in the summer, and we technically went year-round for school. We didn't get out of school or have our school canceled because of "snow days" like public school kids did when they were stuck at home surrounded by snow. Instead, Stella gave us "sun days," where we would go to the pool and enjoy the sunshine rather than work on our lessons for the day. Additionally, I juggled volunteering multiple hours a week at two hospitals and one of the local libraries. I would be applying for scholarships and colleges soon. I wanted to ensure that my applications looked better than the average applicant's so that I could stand a chance at getting accepted into anything.

Stella had been the first person in our family to go to college, and even though she'd only graduated with an associate's degree, it was still a huge accomplishment. She was adamant that I also go to college to have a chance in life.

To gain experience, I volunteered in the outpatient lab at one of the local hospitals, where I sat with phlebotomists all day and passed out surveys to the patients who came in to have their blood drawn. These people were sick but not sick enough to be admitted into one of the hospital beds on one of the upper floors. They had lipomas and cysts on their arms and necks, the growths making them look grotesque and frightening.

I didn't ask anyone about those patients because I didn't want to seem rude, and I was worried about them writing me a bad review for being insensitive. Instead, I kept my mouth shut, worked on my schoolwork when there weren't any patients, and passed out surveys to those who came in.

I was on the physical therapy floor in another hospital where I volunteered, which was much more hands-on. I could talk with patients who had recently had hip or knee replacements and get to know them or provide company. I was able to walk around with them to help them gain back their mobility after their surgeries.

I worked with them in the physical therapy room at the end of the hallway with bands, exercise balls, treadmills, and ellipticals. I brought trays of food to some of the patients and refilled their ice if they needed it.

It was a lot of work, but I was able to help people, and even if only for a few moments, I was able to brighten their day. It solidified my choice to pursue something in the medical field even more.

I also volunteered at the local library, where I was one of the lone teen participants in the summer library programs for my age group. Because of the lack of competition, I was able to win prizes in all the contests in my age group. The prizes were mostly more books, but that was fine with me. I simply added it to my collection.

I used to read as a way to escape. I was especially interested in reading young adult novels that had a happily ever after I could skip to and read over, my heart pounding with desire and a flicker of hope burning in my chest. I often pictured myself in that position, hoping my

prince charming would swoop in and save me from my mess. That I

would get completely swept off my feet, and I would finally be able to

forget the trauma of my past. A girl can dream, right?

Chapter Sixteen: Is This What I Was Made For?

That fall of my senior year of high school, things started changing fast. I first went on college campus visits to WVU-Tech in Montgomery, West Virginia. I started applying to various colleges and for multiple scholarships and grants. I checked out books filled with scholarships that were as thick as my forearm from the library and combed them for any scholarships and grants I could apply for. One of the good things about having a rough childhood is that personal essays for scholarships are a Godsend, as anyone is willing to give money to a young adult who has overcome adversity.

That September, I turned eighteen and had a small get-together with my closest friends in our backyard. Mom came, too, and I remember feeling embarrassed by her because I was worried that Chelsea would think I was a dork or a nerd.

Mom still called me "baby" and pulled me to her and kissed me on the head like you would a child. She had missed out on years of opportunities to do it, so I get it – she was just trying to make up for lost time and experiences. Nothing about our relationship was ever normal – she'd given that part up when she decided to try to hurt me.

Stella would invite Mom to spend time with us for a holiday or one of the kids' birthdays, but I never really knew how to interact with her. It wasn't as easy and comfortable as it should have been. It was awkward as we tried to navigate through the muddled mess. The best way I can explain it is that she was familiar to me, but only in the way that a distant aunt you see once or twice a year is familiar. There was no connection or bond there, and the time to form that bond for it to survive my tumultuous teenage years had passed. It hurt knowing that I would forever go without those moments and that bond that exists only between a mother and her child. I couldn't yet identify what I was missing, but the space left was felt and acknowledged in every interaction with her.

After I turned eighteen, I found that everything was still the same and it bummed me out. Everyone talks about how everything changes when you turn eighteen and you'll have all this freedom. I still felt trapped by the need to meet Stella's expectations and to make them proud.

My identity relied on it, and I built my identity around it. I felt like I couldn't be myself, not knowing who that was, because I feared it wouldn't be acceptable. Journaling was the only outlet to let out all the thoughts I'd kept pent up during the day, so I continued to purge my thoughts daily. I also continued to read a lot. Stella and I met a former midwife-turned-author at a library event who inspired us to read her memoirs from when she was a midwife. This experience inspired me even more to continue on my path to delivering babies, which I chose to pursue in college.

After Simon was born, I stepped up a lot, helping Stella when and how I could with her little boys, who were only just over a year apart. She bragged about how helpful I was to people at church and within our families. I kept doing it more to win her favor. After I finished my schoolwork for the day, I often helped Stella make dinner, and then I helped her feed the little ones. I helped clean up after dinner, and if the baby bottles needed washing, I'd wash those. I bathed the boys, which also involved playing in the bath with them, brushing their teeth, putting lotion on them, and brushing their hair. Then I'd read to them, sing, and rock them until they fell asleep or were close to sleep before laying them down in their crib. I'd end the night downstairs, picking up their toys and putting them all on their shelves and cubbies.

Sometimes, they would want to go to the store or on a date, and I would stay home and watch all three boys. On one of those occasions,

Simon and Shiloh got into a scuffle on the stairs, and I had to reprimand Shiloh as the older sibling. I put Simon down for a late nap shortly afterward, as he was fussy and non-consolable after that incident. He also had not had a nap that day. As always, I rocked and sang to him, but he fought against me in his fussiness. I lightly held his head against my chest to prevent him from banging his head into my chin while he screamed in my face yet again. He eventually fell asleep, and I laid him on his bed blanket. When he woke, he had red fingerprint-sized dots along his temple. I got sick to my stomach at the thought that I did that. *Had I held him down that hard? Maybe Shiloh hurt him more than I'd thought during their scuffle on the stairs?*

I was terrified by what it looked like. I convinced myself that I had caused this, and the idea that I had physically harmed a child that I loved made me want to throw up. *Was I destined to be just like Mom?* I fed Simon some baby cereal since it was close to bedtime, and I'd already put Shiloh and Spencer down for bed. My hands shook as I spooned the thick substance into his mouth, my brain frantically searching for an explanation. If he still looked like this even hours after the incident, he would still look like this when his mom and dad returned. I honestly didn't know what could have caused the indentations on his temple.

When Rory and Stella returned after Simon had fallen back asleep, I decided to come clean because Simon had what looked like fingerprint-sized indentations on the side of his head. I told them I didn't know how they'd gotten there, and Stella immediately looked concerned and alarmed. I frantically tried to explain that maybe it was from when Shiloh pushed his head on the stairs, or it could have been from when I was gently holding Simon in place while I was trying to get him to sleep. She assumed the worst of me, and she blamed me for intentionally hurting her child. She told me she didn't trust me to watch her kids anymore. I was crushed. I hadn't even thought I'd pushed that hard. Maybe that's what Mom had felt, too, in her delusional state – that she wasn't hitting Stella and Abigail that hard when, in reality, she was mercilessly beating them. The indentations were gone when Simon woke up the following day, but the shame and guilt were not.

I felt awful but accepted that maybe Stella was right. Deep down, I was glad to have found out that I was more violent than I realized I was before I could do any more harm. The same could not be said for Mom, as I assumed that nobody had told her that before things got terrible, and she eventually tried to kill me. I felt like no matter how hard I tried, a horrible life was my destiny.

A few weeks later, Stella barged into my room late one night. She grabbed my hand, fell on her knees, and sobbed that she was sorry. I sat up in bed, so confused, as I'd been dead asleep. She explained that she had gotten Simon up that night to feed him and noticed the same indentations I'd described on the side of his face. She checked his bed and saw him lying on a blanket with little ball tassels along the edging. The edging had caused the indentations that night the same way they had the night the last time I'd babysat. So, I didn't hurt him. Shiloh hadn't hurt him under my watch. I'd done nothing wrong. I felt such a relief to know that I hadn't done anything wrong, but I also felt a sense of resentment building up in the pit of my stomach at the idea that she believed I was capable of hurting a child. I know I'd been through a lot in my childhood and had not been a friend to the girls at Mountain Youth Academy while I was there, but I loved Stella's boys like they were my own. I had nightmares about them getting hurt, and it physically hurt me. I felt like all the effort I'd put into impressing her and making her proud of me had been for naught. It was evident that she still thought and expected the worst of me.

After months of begging, that Christmas, Rory and Stella finally got me an acoustic guitar. I was a fan of early Taylor Swift and wanted to learn how to play her songs on the guitar. Her boys were all taking piano lessons, and I was the only one not playing an instrument.

They refused to give me lessons, though, as they said that learning to play the guitar was easy and that most people are self-taught. Never mind the fact that I had no musical background whatsoever. Never mind that it was my senior year, and I didn't have the time to devote to learning how to play the guitar with the workload I was trying to balance while also trying to be as helpful as possible to Stella. I always felt it unfair that they were willing to pay for musical instrument lessons for their boys but not for me. It made me feel inferior and like I wasn't worth the time or effort.

I kept progressing academically, though, as I struggled to learn to play the guitar via rented video lessons from the library and one of the leaders in the teen group who also played guitar. Without actual regular lessons, though, I wasn't getting anywhere. I continued throwing myself into my studies as much as possible as I prepared to wrap up my senior year. I'd gotten into every college I'd applied to and continued to apply for every scholarship and grant I could find.

Since I was homeschooled, the state department didn't trust my transcripts despite earning the test score to earn the coveted PROMISE Scholarship. For that reason, I had to prove that I was smart enough for the PROMISE Scholarship by taking and passing the test given for General Education Degrees or the equivalent of a high school diploma.

Along with the only other homeschool student in the section I worked with, I passed the test with flying colors while everyone else struggled in the classes and practice tests that proceeded to the actual test. I further proved my academic prowess by taking the entrance exam needed to get into some nursing programs for the schools to which I'd applied. I hadn't decided where I wanted to go yet, so I decided to take the test to be covered no matter where I chose. The woman who gave the tests warned me that almost everyone fails the test the first time but that it's a good way to get some experience for the next time. She asked me if I wanted to go ahead and sign up for the next testing session just in case, and I declined. I'd studied and mainly felt confident going into the testing room.

The test included questions about the flow of blood through the heart and what various symptoms could mean for a patient, among other aspects of the human body's function. I passed with flying colors, much to the dismay of the lady at the check-out desk, who seemed impressed that someone as young as me had passed on the first try.

I felt like academics was the only way for me to become anything in life. And I felt like being academically inclined was the magic cure for everything, or at least that's all that mattered.

I hadn't magically been cured from having gone through Mountain Youth Academy. I still had a lot of pain to sift through that I'd ignored. But I buried it as best as possible, lest it wreaked havoc on everything around me.

Chapter Seventeen: Old Habits Die Hard

I was still talking to Andrew occasionally, but I had also caught the attention of someone I used to attend church camp with. He was a few years older than me, so it had been a few years since I'd last seen him. But, just like everyone else, he and I reconnected through Facebook. While Facebook is a good way to connect people socially, some things are better left in the past, and Jordan was one of them.

He messaged me on Facebook after I'd accepted his friend request. I was too nice to ignore someone, but I lapped up the attention when he immediately started flirting with me. I went against my better judgment and against what other girls from camp had done when he'd messaged them in the same way. My insecurities inhibited me from being able to provide a source of validation.

When he found out I was a virgin, things progressed quickly, and I started using my TracPhone to message him for fear that Rory and Stella would read my Facebook messages. I knew they had access to all of my accounts if they wanted to, and with Rory's IT abilities, I knew he'd be able to get access even if he didn't already have it.

Instead, I called him late at night before falling asleep, and he would say things that made me blush in my innocence. I knew it was wrong, but I liked the attention despite the feeling of disgust in the pit of my stomach. He seemed hyper-focused on deflowering me, which was a major red flag that I chose to ignore completely. Instead, I saw it as sweet and endearing because he had also peppered in the pretty language he knew I'd need to hear to make me more likely to accept his proposition. Those are the most dangerous boys to watch out for – the ones who have figured out how to layer the sensual expectations with the promises of forever precisely. This way, women are provided just the right amount of poison to dull our senses before we willingly give ourselves up to the wolves as a lamb for slaughter. And slaughter me, he would have. He was another Brandon looking for self-gratification. I was so desperate to feel special that I couldn't see past his superficial flattery. I let it continue and invited him to my youth group one Wednesday evening to hang out in a church setting.

He was too old to have been in the youth group, as it was for high school-aged kids. But, when the new youth pastor asked how old he was, Jordan lied and said he was still of high school age.

He feared Pastor Clint wouldn't allow him to stay and hang out with me if he'd told the truth. I did my best to impress Jordan that

evening by answering every question I could about the Bible lesson;
being homeschooled and having a Bible class every day paid
off. Afterward, Pastor Clint pulled us aside and told Jordan he knew he
wasn't still in high school and didn't appreciate him lying to him. Jordan
hung his head in shame but admitted to his wrongdoing. Pastor Clint
was also vocal about his disapproval of someone lying to spend time
with me, albeit in a church setting. He also talked to Rory and Stella
about it, and they were surprised that I was still talking to Jordan.

I lied and shrugged it off, stating that he had asked to hang out
with me weeks ago and told him he could at church. I claimed that he
must have found the schedule on the church's website. I talked to Jordan
on the phone whenever I could.

I was a romantic and loved listening to the tenor in someone's
voice, the sound of their laughter, and the way they breathed. Besides,
texting on a TracPhone is tedious; you must repeatedly hit buttons to
type one letter.

I thought I was being slick by only talking to Jordan on the phone
when Stella and Rory weren't around – right after I woke up in the
morning, right before I fell asleep at night, when they were gone, and
when I was home alone watching the boys.

Leave it to me to not even think about the fact that my minutes,
which accumulated every month since I never used them, were now

significantly depleted and thus were evidence of my crime. Jordan had messaged Rory's brother, Rowan, who had been one of Jordan's former camp counselors. He asked Rowan about me and how strict Rory and Stella were – as I had repeatedly claimed they were too strict to let me go out with him like he begged me to. Rowan issued a warning to Rory, stating that Jordan was not a good person. They asked if I was still talking to him, and I denied it. I knew they would disapprove of it, and I was terrified that they'd find out, tarnishing their perception of me.

I'd done a good job deleting mine and Jordan's text messages, so there was no proof. I hadn't even saved his number in my phone for fear of being discovered. I went to great lengths to cover up this secret life that I was living via phone conversations. But in the end, it wasn't enough. Suspecting that there was more to the story,

Stella searched my call history and found the record of an hour-long conversation with someone from an unsaved number. I tried to deny it until the very end, fearing what was to come if the truth came out and trying my best to delay the inevitable.

She finally found out I had talked to Jordan while they were out, and I was caring for the boys. She looked at me with disgust and disappointment and claimed that she could no longer trust me to watch her children and that she would never leave them with me again. She believed I couldn't care for her children because I was on the phone. At this point, I'd already heard it before in an instance where I was not guilty and allowed it to crush my soul completely. This time, it didn't affect me as much.

Instead, the situation just added to the resentment I felt toward Rory and Stella and the fact that any time I tried to be myself and go out and do my own thing, I was reprimanded for it because it was outside of the umbrella of their safety. They made me feel so guilty and ashamed for just talking to someone, even if it was someone I shouldn't be talking to. Rather than let me find out what a pig he was by myself, they shamed me for even trying. I was so frustrated with how poorly they handled the situation that I asked Mom to come and get me.

I'd never reached out to her with such a request before, but she jumped at the opportunity. She had lied to the Department of Health and Human Resources offices for years after they'd approved her for government housing. She had always claimed that I came and stayed with her for weeks sometimes and that I needed a place to stay, so she got a two-bedroom apartment. I threw some of my stuff in a bag and left, much to the dismay of Rory and Stella. I guess they didn't expect me to go. I was just so tired of feeling like a disappointment. I felt like no matter what I did, they would always be disappointed.

No matter how much I helped or stepped up, if I did something they disapproved of and ventured outside their carefully molded box, they berated me for it. It's not like I was sneaking out or planning to meet up with Jordan without their knowing. I simply enjoyed having someone to talk to who wouldn't judge me. I was trying my best, and it wasn't enough. It was then that I realized that it would never be enough. They would always hold my past and who I had been against me. It's as if they were waiting for me to revert back to who I was which inhibited me from growing and learning.

Mom was excited to have me with her, and I enjoyed the peace of not being judged and shamed. I was finally with someone to whom I wasn't a burden because her job was to take care of me.

Rory eventually came to pick me up, and the threat of not finishing high school loomed over me. I decided to return and give it one more try, hoping they would stop suffocating me as much.

The weeks passed, and Stella never left me alone with her kids again. I prepared for the end of my senior year. I was studying hard for my final exams, preparing to showcase my talent for the homeschool graduation – one that I was failing miserably at since I still couldn't play the guitar - and readying for my last homeschool social. I'd decided not to go with anyone this year, as going with Stephen had not worked out the year before and had only made the whole ordeal more stressful since I had to ensure he and I matched as per tradition. I'm unsure what for, though, as we didn't even get any pictures together. I had settled, months prior, on a golden beige dress with a corset bodice and a tulle

ballgown skirt. I tried it on at the second-hand store and felt like a

princess. I'd almost paid off the dress – something I'd done with my

extra money.

One day in late April, I was in my room trying to finish my

homework. I had only ten days of lessons left in my senior year before I

finished high school. I could tell by the sounds upstairs that Stella was

preparing dinner. Knowing my duty and what Stella had come to expect

of me, I went upstairs to help.

I was quiet as I got out the pots and pans needed for the recipe,

and Stella asked what was wrong. I told her that I was hoping to be able

to focus on my homework that evening. In her frustration, she assumed

I was lazy and told me to go downstairs to my room. I returned to my

room and stayed, working on homework until Rory got home.

Rory had barely gotten in the door when Stella started in. I was

sitting on my bedroom floor downstairs, but I could hear her yelling

upstairs to Rory: "She's a piece of trash. She's a waste of space. She's a

waste of God's creation." She was saying these things about me. I was

the only other *she* in the household.

All at once, everything that I'd believed about myself for the 18

years that I was alive was spoken into existence. There was no denying it anymore. No matter how much I tried to cover up the steaming pile that was Destinee, a turd was still a turd. All of my efforts, all the suppressing myself, all the energy I put into trying to prove them wrong about me was for nothing. It was no wonder Mom had wanted to kill me. It was no wonder Brandon had left. It was no wonder Mamaw had wanted me aborted. It was no wonder Ralph had seen me as just a piece of meat. I was worthless. Useless. Pointless. Unloved. Trash.

They left to take Spencer to cello practice without speaking to me. When I heard the garage door close and checked to ensure their minivan was out of the driveway, I called Mom to get me again.

This time, she said her car wasn't working and she would have to borrow a neighbor's car. I was frustrated that a fifty-something-year-old woman didn't have her life together enough to have a working vehicle to pick up her daughter in need, whom she hadn't had to take care of for quite some time.

I was resolute in my decision this time. I couldn't and wouldn't be going back after what Stella said. It was evident what she thought of me, just as it was evident that no amount of bribery or good deeds would ever win me favor with her. I would spend forever stuck under the thumb of trying to win her approval at this rate, and it would both break me down and suffocate me simultaneously. I would never fit in or live up to who or what they wanted me to be.

Mom finally showed up, and I grabbed the little essentials I had packed and left without looking back. Mom was the first person they called when Stella and Rory got home and noticed my absence. I talked to them briefly, and they told me they wouldn't let me finish school if I wasn't back at their house by morning. I told Stella that Mom had to borrow a car to get me, and she replied, "Well, you figured a way out there. I guess you'll figure out a way back."

In a moment of weakness at hearing Stella's voice and feeling the old familiar need to appease her, I asked Mom to take me back. The person she borrowed the car from had gone to bed for the night. So, I grabbed what little belongings I could carry and walked into the dark and rainy night. Mom had threatened to call the police if I left, but I didn't believe her. I also didn't care. I explained to her that I needed to get back to Elkview.

The trip would take me all night, but it was one that I was willing, in my stubbornness, to make. I walked for about ten minutes before it started to rain. My headphones, the only thing pumping the numbing agent of music into my ears, got tangled in my wet gear and were pulled off of me into the mud.

There was no saving them, and I accepted their fate. If only the same could be said for my stubbornness. I walked for another ten minutes before a cop silently pulled behind me and turned on her lights. She stuffed my belongings in her trunk and then made me sit in the back of her car like a criminal. I hadn't done anything wrong. I was trying to right the wrong I had done in leaving by returning by any means necessary.

She drove me back to Mom's apartment complex, and I gave up trying to get back to Elkview. I accepted the fact that this was the choice that I had made, and I would have to live with the consequences.

I would rather live with the consequences than return to how things were. So, I stayed. Stella made her disappointment in me well-known in that she made a big deal out of me no longer graduating and the graduation announcements we ordered being null, void, and pointless. I didn't care.

I was more committed than ever to my decision. I was not going to allow Stella to hurt me again, and I could no longer trust them., When Stella realized that not graduating with a high school diploma didn't bother me since I already had my GED, she told me I could no longer attend the social.

I'd made payments on my dress with my money, I'd already picked it up, and it was hanging in my room at Stella's. I fought her on that, bringing the facts to her attention. She eventually relented and agreed to let me go. However, mom didn't bother to help me get ready like Stella had done the year before.

I was left to do it alone, and it was a mess. I'd burned my neck badly with my curling iron, as I was not very familiar with using the tool correctly. I also could not do my makeup anywhere near as well as the professional at the Clinique counter, so it was not my best moment. And the pale gold dress washed me out since it blended with my pale skin.

I did my best to remain optimistic and make it work because I knew this was my last chance to shine with my fellow seniors before I got spit out into the real world.

In addition to the opportunity for a multiple-course meal and dancing at the country club, seniors were allowed to share their post-high school plans with the group. I shared my plans, which I'd decided based on what I thought Stella wanted and what would make her happy. I recited to the group, my hand shaking as I gripped the microphone with sweaty palms, "I'm going to Pensacola Christian College to become a labor and delivery nurse."

Even as I said those words, focusing on the lights above me instead of the dozens of people before me, I knew that wasn't what I wanted. I could not honestly see myself going to Florida and leaving my life behind.

I'd recently gone on a college visit to Pensacola Christian College in Pensacola, Florida, with a local youth group. It was a strict Christian college campus with a dress code for students and other rules like a curfew, no social media allowed, and no worldly ventures outside of the school were allowed either. They were said to have spies at popular hang-out spots surrounding the campus, like the mall, to monitor PCC students' behavior outside the campus to ensure it reflected Godly behavior.

Stella encouraged me to go there, though I'd gotten into all five colleges I'd applied to. She would have been more at peace knowing the rules would protect me.

The thought of continuing to be smothered, though, scared me. I spent my whole time at Stella's feeling smothered, so much so that, to appease her, I just conformed to what I thought would make her happy based on careful observation. In the process, I lost my sense of identity. Being smothered in college would further inhibit me from figuring out anything for myself out of my habitual conforming to others' expectations to appease them.

I ended the night crying outside in one of the many little gazebos in the country club courtyard. Some of the girls had ventured out to check on me. To explain to them why I was in my situation, I had to tell them my back story, which I'd done so often that I almost had it memorized at this point.

I was comfortable sharing it because it was my story and because people were usually too shocked by what they heard to dig into who I was. Or it acted as a proactive justification for why I was the way I was. I explained to them what Stella had said and that I would no longer be graduating with them.

They hugged me and sympathized with me. I was so embarrassed that my life was so chaotic. They had functional familial units and knew precisely where they were headed. And my life was in pieces, just as it had always been and would seemingly always be.

Chapter Eighteen: Generational Curses Die Even Harder

After moving back in with Mom, I contacted Andrew, who indicated he was single. We texted and messaged daily, and I fell back into something familiar and comfortable amid the chaos and upheaval of my life. I craved security and consistency in the madness. Even though he was not a strong foundation, I clung to him in desperation. I held on to the promise that we would get married after he returned from Basic Training, where he would be in a couple of weeks. I felt pressured to fit an entire relationship within those few weeks, as I was worried he'd forget me or see me as a waste of time otherwise.

We would talk on the phone every single night before bed, but it wasn't often for very long. He always used work as an excuse for why he would get off the phone after only talking with me for a few minutes. And no, I'm not being a dramatic teenage girl. Most of the time, it was only a few minutes, usually about ten.

He would claim he was too tired to talk anymore and would go to bed. An hour later, he would still be posting on Facebook, and I would be infuriated because I knew he was lying, and it was apparent. But I wouldn't call him out because I was desperate to be loved and afraid he would leave me. After all, I'd proven to be so unlovable already.

He lived an hour and a half from where I resided with Mom, and she didn't have the gas money to drive me there. I was now getting the monthly Social Security money Rory and Stella had been getting for me. To prove my eligibility for the supplemental income, I had to take some tests and talk to some people about *how things were on my worst day*. After the therapists and doctors heard my story, they were practically throwing money at me. I used that money to fill Mom's gas tank so she could drive me to Oak Hill, West Virginia. I was determined to prove my loyalty to him before he left for Basic Training by giving him all of me, the parts I'd almost frivolously given away a few too many times for my liking. In my naivety, I convinced myself that if I gave him my innocence, he would always love me and want to be with me. He'd have to. Right? That's the way it was supposed to work. I convinced myself it would come true if I believed in it enough.

Andrew and I decided on a day and time to meet and spend time together before he left for Basic Training. I eagerly counted the days until our union was forever consecrated and finalized. I was desperate for us to work out. I felt like the entire future of my happiness rode on his being with me. That morning, I got up early and scrubbed myself to make a good first impression. I flat ironed my hair against my head, trying to fight the volume that my natural curl brought. Mom smoked the whole way there, and I flipped through the radio stations until I landed on a song I wanted. She knowingly and willingly led her lamb to slaughter. I distracted myself by listening to the radio and looking out my window. I didn't want to think about what would come because I didn't want to set any standard, and then Andrew let me down.

We pulled into the Oak Hill Library parking lot, which had been the designated meeting spot. He walked up to the car, his blue eyes shining and a smile on his face. He was so handsome that I wanted to melt into my seat. I didn't care that we were currently sitting in Mom's black car or that it was literally on its last leg. All that mattered was him.

I shoved a quick goodbye to Mom and marched off with Andrew. He had walked from his house to the library, so we were stuck walking back.

He kissed me, touched my hips, held my hand, and promised me the world. And I, like so many women throughout history before me, fell for it. *Hard.* I was blinded by love and by the possibility of a stable future. And by those blue, blue eyes rimmed by long lashes and thick dark brows. I was mesmerized.

He took this opportunity to drop the bomb, and he still had drawings hanging above his bed that said *Chelsey loves Andrew,* but he just hadn't had time to take them down. I was so desperate for us to work that I didn't bother speaking up about it. I knew it didn't make sense. *What do you mean you haven't had time? It takes two seconds to rip down a poster.* But I smiled and nodded, doing my best to play the part of the dumb and in love girl. I was worried that if I spoke up and he caught a glimpse of just how dangerously insecure I was, he'd run for the hills.

After a short walk, we ended up where he claimed he was currently crashing. When I asked why he wasn't living with his mom, with whom I'd been in contact already unbeknownst to him, he said it was because she kicked him out.

I found that hard to believe based on what little l did know about her. Like I did with everything he told me, I went along with it so as not to cause a fuss.

When we got to his friend Suzanne's (her parents' house, as she was still a teen), I said a quick *hello* before Andrew led me into his room, and they all headed out the door. His mattress was on the floor, and his clothes covered the rest since his laundry basket overflowed. He tried to scoop them off the floor and into the basket. Like, he couldn't have cleaned up before I got there? Is anyone keeping track of the red flags here?

He immediately initiated what I'd come all this way for. I hesitated for a second before his blue eyes looked into mine, and I trusted him to take care of me and prove all the men before him wrong. And I couldn't help but notice the "Chelsey loves Andrew" crayon drawings on black construction paper hanging on the wall above me. I thought about reaching up and ripping them down.

Afterward, he grabbed my left hand, pointed to my ring finger, and told me that he would put a ring on that finger when he got back from Basic. Even though he said it without much conviction, I believed him because I wanted so badly for it to be true. My heart swelled with the possibility that my future fate was sealed. I didn't have to wander from one place to the next. My future was in Andrew, or so I thought.

Later, we rode bikes to the bowling alley where he worked. He introduced me to his co-workers, who sized me up like a piece of meat.

I couldn't even bring myself to look either of them in the eyes because I feared what I'd find there. I could smell their insatiable hunger for female flesh dripping from their drool and sweat already. He chatted with his buddies while I walked to the bathroom to pee. I should have been happy to have finally taken that step, but my chest felt like it was full of cement. I wanted to cry, not tears of joy, but tears of sadness at what I'd lost and so frivolously given up in hopes of making someone stay.

I'd spent my whole life resenting Mom for how desperate she was, and here I was, acting more and more like her every single day. I forced a smile on my face, willing myself to feel it. I looked at my smile in the mirror, but I didn't dare look myself in the eyes. I couldn't bring myself to. I was too ashamed of what I'd done and scared of what I'd find if I locked eyes with my reflection. I knew Andrew had brought me here to show me off to his buddies because he was bragging about what a *hot, easy bang* I was or whatever lingo guys used back then. I was too scared and too much of a coward to admit that they were right. I was just an easy lay, desperate to be loved. I knew right then, when I stepped out of the bathroom and looked at Andrew in the blacklight of the bowling alley, that he didn't love me. That this was all for show and to use me.

"Are you ready to head back?" Andrew asked, turning away from his friends, who were still undressing me with their eyes.

I nodded, and we hopped back on the bikes. Andrew showed me through town a bit, and I griped almost the whole time about how badly my thighs hurt from pedaling the bike. I wasn't used to it, and my thighs were on fire. He seemed adamant about speeding ahead of me, and I struggled to keep up. I felt like he was playing games with me - like cat and mouse - because he enjoyed the chase so much. And again, I was desperate enough to fall for it. I was desperate enough to continue chasing him. When we got back, I sat on his bed, with his head in my lap, and we talked about the future. He promised me that we would get married shortly after he returned from Basic at the end of the summer. He told me about the money he would get upon his return and how we could use it for our wedding.

Worried that he'd forget about me while he was away, I asked: "And you're sure you'll be able to write me, and I'll be able to write to you?"

Andrew nodded, rubbing his hand on my thigh.

"What about calls, texts, and that stuff?"

He shook his head no while he played with my hands.

"Can I come see you graduate?" I asked, hopeful that his answer of *I don't know* had changed.

"Actually," he sat up to lay it on me quickly, I guess, "you have to have a driver's license to come visit. I'm sorry," he said, gazing up at me with his blue eyes. I'd always had a thing for boys with blue eyes.

I wanted so badly for it to be true. I knew that it wasn't. None of it was. Still, I listened to Andrew with a dumb smile on my face.

Desperation will do that to you: it turns off your sense of awareness so that you don't acknowledge the fragility of what's to come and don't recognize the consequences of your decisions. I was so hell-bent on being loved that I failed to see the reality of the situation.

When it was finally time for me to meet Mom at the library, Andrew had Suzanne's mom drop me off before she drove Andrew to work. He had given me one of his tie-dye Bob Marley t-shirts that still smelled like him and an Air Force beanie he'd gotten when he enlisted. I meant to take pictures, but I felt I had come across as desperate enough as it was, so I needed to reel it in, lest he see me for who I truly was: a pathetically insecure and lonely girl desperate for love and validation.

If he were to see that, he'd indeed run - far, far away. And I couldn't handle that. I'd built my life around him, and I wouldn't withstand it all crashing down around me. I kissed him repeatedly as Mom waited patiently, cigarette in one hand and car keys in the other.

Finally, I let him go, and I sat down in the passenger seat of Mom's junky old car. I had read so many stories and books before about girls' first times and how they felt so unique and magical and changed. I didn't feel any of that. I felt empty, as if I had just frivolously given away my favorite CD or something vital.

Mom awkwardly asked how it went, and I focused on his promise to marry me. She, of course, wanted to see the ring, which, of course, I could not provide. I explained the situation, and Mom seemed to understand. Or maybe she saw through Andrew's crap already. I asked her again not to say anything to Stella about what I did. I still valued her view of me, whatever I had left to hang on to.

I was deep in thought the rest of the way home, imagining my wedding. Where would it be? Who would we invite? What would I wear? I spent that evening and the next few weeks in the breezeway of Mom's apartment complex, laid out on the bench, scrolling through wedding gowns and saving everything I liked to a Pinterest board.

I also talked to Mom about practicing for my driver's test since I'd already passed it and earned my learner's permit twice since it had expired the first time. I convinced myself I still had time to get it together to fly down to Texas in August and see Andrew graduate from Basic Training.

In the days leading up to his departure, his communication became sparse. It may have been because he was packing his things and fulfilling his responsibilities. I, however, was convinced that he was cheating on me. I'd send a follow-up message if I didn't hear from him for some time. It got on his nerves, but I couldn't help myself. I needed that constant reassurance, that constant reminder that he was still there and he still loved and wanted me.

And then he was off, and communication came to a standstill. I had to trust that all he had told me was true, but that's not what happened. I continued to stalk his Facebook and noticed that he was commenting on friends' posts on his Facebook wall. He told me he wouldn't be able to get on Facebook.

Finally, Andrew contacted me via snail mail, and I got his address from his envelope. I poured out my heart to him in my letters, writing to him as if I were writing in a journal, which I hadn't done since I'd gotten to Mom's. His letter was pretty short. He said he missed me and couldn't wait for "you know what" whenever he returned, which I assumed was code for getting married.

Chapter Nineteen: Self-Harm Comes in Many Forms

Then I got the news that Rory's Mamaw Long, the family's beloved matriarch, had preceded into glory at 92. The news deeply affected and saddened me because his family had become so much my own. But I still wasn't on speaking terms with Rory and Stella, so the thought of attending a funeral with them filled me with anxiety, even more so because I was also walking down the wrong path.

Meanwhile, I attended Mamaw Long's funeral and had all the people I was sure Stella was bad-mouthing me to surround me. I felt their judgment's perceived or actual weight on me during the service. Pastor Baker choked up preaching about how Mamaw Long was willing to serve the church and God with everything she had until the end. I admired her courage and her love for God, though I had accepted that there was no way I'd ever be able to relate.

There was no way God would ever love me like He had loved her.

I was too bitter and too broken. I clung to Rory's second cousin, Lexi, who was closer to my age, during the funeral. She and I were pretty close, and I wasn't comfortable talking to anyone else without being approached first. I was too scared of being turned away or yelled at.

I looked down at Mamaw Long's body in the casket and couldn't help but notice how at peace she looked. She looked natural, like I'd imagined people to look in death, even after the mortician made them up, postmortem, to put on display. I had an intrusive thought to climb into the casket with her and cuddle her. She looked so peaceful and at ease, and as always, my life seemed to be in upheaval. I craved the peace and tranquility Mamaw Long seemed to have found in death, and I wished to absorb some of her peace. It's unbelievable what stress will do to your brain.

I stepped out to use the restroom at one point after the service was over while I waited for Mom to come pick me up. I realized I'd left my purse in the sanctuary. I said hello to Rory's younger brother and his wife. I passed Rory and Stella on my way into the sanctuary, who I then realized had witnessed the whole interaction. I ducked my head in shame, guilt, and anger and hoped to keep them from saying anything to me. Once I retrieved my purse from one of the front pews, I returned the way I came.

In a loud voice for everyone to hear, even though Rowan and his wife were *right there*, Rory said, "Well, at least she can say hi to you guys!" Rory and Stella glared at me as I ducked my head and walked by, disappearing into the safety of Mom's car. I was so embarrassed by them painting this awful picture of me. I didn't feel it was justified, but I didn't feel like I had any grounds to stand and defend myself. So, I kept my mouth shut.

I hitched a ride with Rory's cousin Carrie, whose daughter, Lexi, I was close with, and her family to Mamaw Long's burial since it was further out of town. Lexi and I hiked up the hill in our heels, giggling because we were each falling over rocks and divets in the path. We weren't being obnoxious or anything to disrupt the solemn moment. The preacher said a few final prayers and shared words of comfort with the surviving family members. Once the machine lowered Mamaw Long's casket into the ground, we all wandered off in our separate directions. I stuck with Lexi as we would meet her dad in his truck at the bottom of the hill. We linked arm-in-arm as we stomped down the hill in our heels.

Then I heard the unfamiliar growl of Rory's vocalized anger directed at me, "How dare you show up to my grandmother's funeral like it's some joke to you."

Lexi and I stopped in our tracks, and I turned around, baffled.

Rory must have gotten enough of a reaction from the puzzled

look on my face to prompt him to continue, "You come here and laugh and play around like it's all some joke. You weren't even her family." At this point, Stella started to pull on Rory, who was obviously grieving.

There it was again. The reminder that I didn't belong to any family or that I didn't fit in anywhere. I didn't let anyone see how much it affected me, though. I held my head high and turned with Lexi as we continued down the hill to her dad's truck, which was already running. I hopped in behind Lexi, apologizing to her dad, Wendell, for the delay. Lexi immediately went into recalling the scene that had just unfolded. They were all baffled as well. I tried to play it cool, as if I was unbothered by it. My strategy worked because they eventually dropped the topic altogether.

Meanwhile, Mom was in the market for a new (to her) car, as the pieces of junk she had never lasted long. Mamaw Goldie, Mom's mom, came over one day, stating she would help Mom buy a car. She also helped Mom scour the newspaper ad bulletin for people selling used cars.

Mom called about all of them, and Mamaw sat beside her, prompting Mom about which questions to ask next and when to show interest. It was a weird dynamic to see between mother and adult child. It was strange to see how helpless Mom was and how dependent she was on her, despite how awful Mamaw had been to her. We drove to the various opportunities for cars. She finally settled on an old black car with ashtrays and a touch screen. What a juxtaposition of items outside of their timeline.

Mom was like a child with a new toy. She spent as much time as she could on the road, showing off her new wheels to anyone looking. Even if she had no reason to be out, she'd stop at the gas station for some Reese's and a Pepsi or at the local thrift store to check for good deals. Even if it meant she was using the last two dollars she had to last the remaining two weeks of the month, Mom put the money in the gas tank so she could drive around town. She'd done this for years and was unfazed by the continuous cycle.

I realized I wanted a job to earn money since Mom was stingy and frivolous with hers. I also focused on getting my license so I could see Andrew for his graduation in August. I finally tasted freedom and desperately gulped it down, wanting more. I landed the job at Foodland with ease, and because I was over eighteen, they put me back in the deli with another new girl around the same age as me. Everyone else in the department was either elderly or heavily addicted to pills.

West Virginia has sadly often been labeled the least happy state in America, so this is no surprise. I couldn't see it then because of my immaturity and naivety, but people get stuck in this muck of depression that makes them reach out for pills, drugs, alcohol, food, and whatever else they can get their hands on to fill the void. These addictions inhibit them from seeing a way out. They're just unhappy and lost. And it's so easy to get sucked into that. Especially as an eighteen-year-old girl who was just now free enough to figure out who she was and what she wanted out of life. That's what I was supposed to figure out now, right? According to the way the world told me to do things.

My old youth pastor came to visit me at some point during this transition in my life, and he expressed his apprehension about my decision and his worry for my future. I internally rolled my eyes, as teenagers do, and assured him that all was well. I was happy and all taken care of, and that's all that mattered. I was even going to church. I still believed in God and did everything I was supposed to do to make myself look good - like I was living the part. The reality could not have been further from the truth.

Especially after I got news from Andrew's mother that she would fly down to Texas with Andrew's girlfriend, Chelsey, to see him graduate in August. She expressed her condolences for delivering the heartbreaking news.

I'd reached out via Facebook message and introduced myself to his mom as his fiancé just weeks earlier, and she had expressed her excitement for us both. Now, she got to watch and participate in her son's utter obliteration of my heart.

I know I was foolish to put so much faith and trust in an individual who had let me down so many times, but I wanted it to work out badly. Even though all the signs of his cheating were there, I was reluctant to believe them. I put my faith and hope in him and was taken aback when he let me down. I worried nobody else would find me worth loving otherwise.

Instead of letting anyone see how heartbroken and embarrassed I was, I set fire to his Air Force beanie and took pictures while it took forever to burn. I felt like a regular Taylor Swift, declaring Andrew as just another beanie to burn (instead of a picture).

I put up my walls, refusing to let anyone see the chaos inside my head. I set forth on my usual path of destruction that was now undeterred by any real supervision. I flirted with all the boys at work - and there were plenty of them - in the meat department, the produce department, the cashiers, the baggers, the stock crew.

I was fresh meat, and I was pretty, and those are the two things that lustful, worldly boys care about. You won't get their attention with your intellect or faith in Jesus. All the other female employees were either older women or high school girls who had already been run through by all the eligible (and even some of those who weren't eligible) young men in Sissonville.

And so, they all flocked back to the deli counter to flirt with me over a free chocolate chip or sugar cookie meant for kids aged twelve and under. No matter their morals or values, all men are easily enticed with food. I lapped up the attention and the compliments. Even though it made me feel icky at the end of the day, it did give a brief dose of dopamine while also briefly bandaging the daddy wound.

All the while, I was trying to figure out who I was in the midst of all this. I had been suppressed for so long and made to feel like I had to please Stella to be in her favor. I didn't know who Destinee was or what I wanted in life.

That summer, I experimented with everything I'd been sheltered from in my journey to figure out who I was and what I liked. Not only was I trying to fit in, but I was attempting to find the antidotes to my emotional and mental turmoil.

And each thing - engaging in casual sex, smoking weed behind the dumpster at work, snorting pills in the walk-in freezer, getting drunk in the backseat of my co-workers' car - brought me further and further from the peace and joy that I was so desperately searching for.

I couldn't understand why people got addicted to these feelings. I didn't feel any better afterward, and I'm ashamed that I didn't remember enough of the event to say one way or the other. After a particularly low weekend out, I remember coming home to Mom and John's apartment and letting the scalding hot water of the shower run over me. I was trying to wash away the shame and the guilt that I felt, and no matter how badly the water burned my skin, I still felt so dirty and gross. I felt used and cheap. I felt broken and lonely. But my brain could not comprehend that this feeling was going to remain no matter how hard I tried to fill the void with the carnal desires of my flesh. My feelings were unquenchable. I was the poster child for a stereotypical girl with daddy issues. And I hated myself for it.

Chapter Twenty: Not a Moment Too Soon

I had spent the summer enjoying my freedom too much, not realizing I was on a dangerous path of self-destruction. Later that summer, after we'd made attempts to fix the broken relationship, Stella dragged me to sign up for classes at the local community college for fear that I was throwing away my entire future by taking a year off. I'd lose all my scholarships and grants, which I'd worked hard to earn. The data on how few students pursue a college degree if they take a year off after high school is astonishing. She convinced me that getting an education would set me up for life. So I went, still as desperate as ever to please her and make her love me again. Rory and Stella had taken me to buy a laptop with the money I'd earned from work.

A few weeks after I started working at Foodland, one of the cashiers at the front introduced himself to me. I entertained him, as I did most of the boys I worked with then. I kept them all at arm's length, making excuses for why we couldn't hang out outside of work or why I couldn't be their girlfriend.

But Easton was so persistent that he used to have his mom drive him to the grocery store even on days he wasn't working so that we could hang out on my break. Other girls might have found it sweet and endearing, but I found it annoying, which is surprising considering how much I craved attention from the opposite sex.

Easton was a couple of years younger than me, and his attempts to impress me got on my nerves more than anything, but I kept him on standby for any dry spells when I wasn't getting enough attention to fill the bottomless pit I required to function.

Desperate for attention and love, Easton chased me relentlessly. He believed me when I gave him my rubbish of an excuse that I wanted to focus on college instead of being in a relationship. I wasn't worried about my studies or interested in him. He called me "baby," which reminded me of Mom and how she couldn't accept that I'd grown up.

Things were getting more tense each day at Mom's, as I did whatever I wanted whenever I wanted because I was eighteen, legally an adult, and no longer under the thumb or rule of anyone.

Mom couldn't control me – we hadn't developed the normal mother-daughter relationship, nor had we developed a strong foundation built on trust and respect as most parents have with their children. I saw her as broken and pathetic.

I was allowing all the resentment toward Mom to bubble to the surface and spill over into yelling and screaming fights with her. I was finally able to release all the pain and trauma, albeit in a very unhealthy way. As feisty as ever, Mom fought back with just as much vengeance. All the guilt and shame she had collected over the years by not being able to raise me turned into a venom that she spewed at me with her words, too. I was on a rampage, and nobody could stop me. I was desperate to numb the pain and fit in with someone, so I didn't care about how it was affecting anything or anyone else.

Rory and Stella had told me to tell Mom my laptop was a loan from Rory, so Mom was less likely to try to sell it out from under me as vengeance. On the final evening, I was at Mom's, and she took the laptop to ensure it returned to them, who she believed were the rightful owners. When I came to retrieve it, I found she'd put knives in the door from the inside so that I couldn't get inside even after I unlocked it. I was young and pretty strong, so I just pushed on the door a bit, and it gave. Mom was appalled and acted like I'd just broken in, which is precisely what she told the cops when they showed up.

One of her neighbors from the same building had heard the commotion and called the cops. That's one of the downfalls of apartment complexes - everyone knows everyone's business because sound bounces off the walls in the breezeways.

The cops were annoyed at being called out over a simple

domestic dispute when there were more important things to deal with. In their annoyance, they threatened that they would take one of us away in handcuffs if they were called back out for us. I decided it was best if I left. I'd burned all my bridges. I was homeless, and I didn't know where else to go.

I rode with Mom's neighbor, Robin, to her church. She was going to clean it that evening, and I offered to help to get out of the house while I figured out my next moves. While helping her, the idea of calling Easton and asking to stay with him until I figured things out randomly crossed my mind. I was out of options, and my brain hurt from trying to develop ideas. I climbed to the top of the church's driveway in an attempt to get enough cellphone service to call him.

Cars whizzed by me, and I was mortified because I convinced myself they could see the mess I was just by looking at me. Easton called me back shortly after that and told me his mom had, with great hesitation and reservation, agreed to let me stay with them for a couple of weeks. I was incredibly relieved.

Robin and I met Easton and his older brother at Foodland. I loaded up all we could fit in the truck's bed after we got to Mom's apartment. Once everything was said and done, we set off to my new beginning. I was eager for things to get better.

Their mom's house was gorgeous and huge, considering I'd come from a tiny apartment and would now stay in a four-story home. Josh, Easton's older brother, parked their dad's truck, and we headed inside. I felt like I had a clean slate and a chance to start over.

I introduced myself to Easton's mom and dad, Tessa and Jake. The two were divorced but still together. They lived in separate houses, though, because they couldn't stand to be around each other. I was desperate for somewhere to rest while trying to make sense of the mess in my life. I felt so alone in this world.

Nobody wanted me, and nobody loved me. I felt the exhaustion from the stress in my life in my bones. I longed to curl up under a warm blanket, close my eyes, and never wake up.

That night, after we had homemade hamburgers for dinner, thanks to Tessa, who had proven to be an excellent cook,

I lay down on Easton's futon in the room that was supposed to be the office. He had moved his television and Xbox into it and now used the futon as a bed. He had a perfect bedroom upstairs but preferred the room away from everyone. After Tessa turned all the lights off and everyone was ready to go to bed, Easton left to lie on the couch in the living room, as per Tessa's request.

I sat up, feeling wholly despondent and worried about what would happen if I were left alone with my thoughts to torture me. I asked Easton to stay, and I saw the outline of his body illuminated by the dim light of the lamps in the living room. He hesitated and then walked back into the room before crawling onto the futon behind me. I scooted back into him, eager to feel a human connection, and he wrapped his arms around me. Despite everything I'd been through, I was able to fall asleep.

He had to get up and go to school the next day, where he was a sophomore at the local high school. Tessa didn't trust me to be alone in her house, and rightfully so, since I was still a stranger.

I got up with them and waited to catch the city bus, which I'd been riding to and from class already, at the local McDonald's since not many other businesses were open at 6:30 in the morning.

I saved up money and looked for somewhere to live, much to the encouragement of Tessa, who had already had a bad experience taking in one of Easton's friends. She didn't want to grow to care about and take care of someone only to be abandoned again. I could understand that.

I started to open up to Easton like I did everyone else - giving him the usual spiel of where I'd come from. He boldly shared that he'd been with so many girls that he'd lost count. As selfish as it was, a part of me died a little inside. I was also disgusted by his having been around so much, especially since he was only sixteen years old. All I could think about was how I would measure up to all the girls before me. I seemed to be doing a pretty crappy job at measuring up to anyone's standards and expectations of me.

I worried that if I didn't measure up, he'd toss me to this side, and I'd be left to figure things out again. I had developed a severely lacking sense of self-confidence that was entirely dependent on verbal reassurance from my male counterparts.

I was jealous of anyone and anything that stole his attention for even the briefest of moments. I went against my better judgment and slept with him, hoping that would be enough to make him want to stay. While juggling class and a young life crisis, I found a little studio apartment right down the road from Tessa's house.

I'd gotten so many scholarships and grants that I was getting money back each semester to go to school. I could use that money to pay my bills, and I was working, so I would have money coming in. The apartment was right off the main road, so I could continue to catch the city bus to and from school easily.

Tessa helped me complete the paperwork, and we made the deposit. I was so eager to please her that I went along with it even though I was terrified. Then, seeing how attached Easton was to me, Tessa changed her mind. She decided it wasn't a good idea for me to be out alone like that, especially as young as I was. She said that I could stay with her and pay rent every month. I agreed because being alone scared me – I'd seen what I could do, which was not good. I couldn't be trusted to care for myself and didn't want to be left alone to my own devices.

Easton and I started officially dating, and I latched onto him, holding on for dear life that this would be the fix I needed for all my problems. I fell in love with the idea of him and the security that idea offered. I lapped up the constant attention and affection, trying to convert the currency to equate to the love and acceptance I needed. For the most part, the almost constant physical attention was enough to make me feel loved, though I was still confusing lust and desire with love. Lust is much more tangible than love - you can see, smell, taste, and feel it. Real love is much more difficult to recognize, especially for someone who has seldom been shown love. It was close enough to love for me, or so I convinced myself.

I cared about him as a person, but looking back, I was never in love with him. I needed someone to take care of me; he still relied on his mom to take care of him – only I was now filling that role. We were a toxic match made in heaven. Easton's older brother, Josh, had overshadowed him his whole life, and he would be in a popular MTV television series based in the area. Josh had always been more outgoing, had better grades, got more attention, and was better at sports.

Easton chased Josh's shadow his whole life but could never live up to the perceived expectations of their parents. Easton kind of gave up and caved in on himself. He had developed a victim mentality and saw everything as a personal attack. I was overly jealous and worried that he was going to cheat on me or give someone else his attention, and he would easily fall in love with them when he realized I wasn't worth the time and effort. I was projecting. I had severe attachment issues that inhibited me from developing authentic connections with people, so I fell in and out of love with the idea of almost anyone, seeing what they could all offer me to help me feel secure. I was worried he was the same way and assumed the worst, as I'd come to expect from people at this point.

Easton eventually confessed to me that he had been a virgin before me. I was relieved in one aspect because I was jealous of all the invisible girls I competed with in my head.

In another aspect, though, I was furious that he'd lied to me about something so important for so long. I should have known because I'd brought it up quite a bit over the months prior.

I was insecure, and the unknown details were eating at me and driving me crazy. *Exactly how many? Who? What were their names? What did they look like? How old were they? Where was it? What do you remember?* When he couldn't answer these questions, I filled in the gaps with the worst-case scenarios in my constantly anxious state.

Initially, he'd told me he'd lost count, then he told me it was fewer than fifty girls. The number kept dropping over the coming months until it was fewer than a dozen and then none. If he was willing to lie so easily about something as monumental as this, I figured he was willing to lie about basically anything. Even though I didn't trust him or feel secure in our relationship because of the lies, I stayed because I believed I wouldn't find anyone else to love me.

When I realized I wouldn't be moving again, I used my extra scholarships and grants to buy a mattress, box spring, bedframe, dresser, and armoire. After we retrieved the rest of my stuff from Mom's house, I set everything up in Tessa's basement to look like a little apartment. It was much more spacious than the little office room Easton and I had been sleeping in. We had a bedroom area, a living room area with some of Tessa's old couches, and a little kitchen area with Easton's mini fridge.

Easton watched movies and television shows when he wasn't playing video games. We would go out on dinner dates frequently or go shopping. Tessa commented that he wasn't as depressed as he used to be since he and I had been together. Easton even told me that he always sat in his little room and played video games before I came along. That made me feel good, like I was contributing something good to someone's life for once.

I fell into Easton's habits of being a couch potato and being inside a lot because I was depressed, too. I didn't have to fake it anymore to make anyone happy, and I figured he'd be more likely to accept me if I conformed to him. I still didn't know who I was because I was busy trying to please everyone else.

Because his depression also made him a people-pleaser, he conformed to my materialism and love for things. No sooner than our paychecks hit our bank accounts, we'd go to Walmart for a midnight run to blow it all on stuff we wanted but didn't need. Like Mom, I'd never experienced true joy and equated the fleeting happiness brought upon by fulfilling a desire as being the next best thing.

Chapter Twenty-One: Two Too-Broken People

I'd started to see a therapist around this time because the thought of becoming like Mom, now that I was getting older, scared the life out of me. I knew that I was entering the incubation period for schizophrenia to rear its ugly head at me and would be stuck in said incubation period from age eighteen to thirty. I'd done my research; I knew that the disease was highly hereditary, and I knew that trauma could cause it to increase in risk. The odds were stacked against me. It was all I could think about. I became terrified to ever have children or a family because it felt inevitable that I would hurt them in some way – the same way Mom had all those years ago. I didn't want that, but I didn't know how to avoid it. The dream of a "normal" life seemed far out of reach. Easton didn't understand my anxiety, nor was he mature or self-aware enough to help me.

I carried that burden with me for a long time, despite the reassurances of my therapist. She even wrote down some reminders for me to meditate on until the symptoms showed up - if they ever did. She

reminded me that I could still have an everyday life with a treatment

plan and medication. I'd seen how well that *didn't* work out for Mom, so

that didn't help much to alleviate my fears. Easton tried to assure me

multiple times that he would make sure I took my medication if I did

develop schizophrenia. I wasn't inclined to believe him. He had no idea

what he was up against - he hadn't witnessed it like I had.

Because I didn't trust him, I went through Easton's phone to see

what else he was lying to me about, and found, multiple times, that he'd

been watching porn. Rather than owning up to his mistakes and

admitting that he lied, he made an excuse each time. *Josh got on his

phone and looked it up. Someone must have hacked his YouTube

account and watched the video.*

He got better and better at hiding that he watched it, and I got

better and better at finding it. The first time it happened, MTV was at

the house filming for *Buckwild,* and I stumbled across evidence from

Easton's search history. I'd borrowed his phone to work on my college

English homework while my phone was on charge.

After I found it and saw how defensive and unwilling he was to

take responsibility, I was ready to walk away from the relationship

altogether. He kept denying it, his pride inhibiting him from being honest. I was adamant that I deserved better. Betrayal burned in my gut – I was giving Easton everything he wanted, so I couldn't understand why he'd search elsewhere. I took his betrayal personally. From my perspective, he chose fake girls with fake bodies who I would never in a million years measure up to on the other side of the screen over me. I couldn't understand why, yet again, I wasn't enough. When I reached out to Tessa for guidance, assuming she'd agree with me since she was also a woman and felt the pressure from the media to be "perfect", she took his side instead. She insisted that watching porn was normal and to be expected from a man in a relationship. She indicated that Easton's wandering eye was something I should just put up with and encouraged me to watch it with him. I was floored.

Not that I was walking on the right path in my Christian faith in the slightest, but I'd grown up memorizing verses at church camp every summer about the lust of the flesh and the eyes and how adultery is committed in the heart first.

It felt too much like he had cheated on me, but nobody else seemed to agree with me. It seemed like Easton's family was starting to see the cracks in the façade I presented and realized that I wasn't this put-together person I presented. Events like these were usually my cue to run away, lest they see how unlovable I was.

Tessa and Jake included me in all their family get-togethers, and although I was quiet and reserved, his family seemed to like me. Tessa's

and Jake's families are enormous, and self-assured people within their

families constantly surrounded me. I'd never been surrounded by so

many people who had lived normal, non-traumatizing lives. It

intimidated me because I was so unsure of who I was. I didn't know how

to adjust to fit in and please them to win their favor, which was not a

manipulation tool but more of a survival technique. It made a lot of

them uncomfortable because they found my shyness unsettling. I was

afraid to say the wrong thing and make them hate me. I was trying so

hard to fit in - I was trying so hard to be someone they saw as worthy.

Within a few months, Easton told me he had fallen in love with

me, and I'd told him I loved him, too. I started talking about my future,

and before long, he was including himself in those things. I allowed it to

happen, confident he would kick me to the curb if I turned him down. I

also found security in both of us planning for our future.

I introduced him to Rory and Stella, which was a huge step

forward for me. I finally acknowledged with them that I was growing up

and moving past their influence. Spencer, Shiloh, and Simon

immediately took to Easton because he was like their new fun uncle who

rough-housed and played Legos with them.

I attended my college classes for a year, and he attended his high

school classes. The following September, he picked me up from my last class of the day to celebrate our one year of being together at our favorite restaurant. I only half noticed that something was abuzz in the air.

He asked what I would expect from a proposal and questioned whether a bent knee would be necessary. I was distracted, scrolling through social media on my phone while he drove us to our destination, and I just agreed to whatever he was up for, not thinking anything of it. We'd discussed it before, and I knew he was currently making payments on a ring we'd picked out at one of the local chain jewelry stores. As far as I knew, he had quite a few payments left to go, and we were nowhere close to getting engaged soon.

He acted strange the whole way to the restaurant and continued to do so after we'd been seated and given our menus. As usual, I was focused inward – toward myself.

I was genuinely surprised when he pulled out a small velvet box and unveiled the small single stone. I said yes without thinking. I felt excited for my future because I had this false hope that, now that I was getting married and going to college, it meant I had my life together and would be fine. As if checking all of these boxes would prevent me from falling apart emotionally and mentally. If only that were true.

Tessa's sister passed away later that month after a long battle with COPD. I resented Tessa's grief because she was an adult, and all I saw was Mom and her unwillingness to handle anything on her own.

Shouldn't they be able to handle it on their own? I did what everyone

else had done when I was grieving - I left her alone. She had always been

so independent that I didn't consider the implications. I didn't analyze

why or how she'd become that way. I was incredibly unforgiving of

everyone else but expected everyone else to shower me with forgiveness

and grace for my shortcomings.

Later that night, after Easton and I had gone to bed, she stumbled

down the basement stairs, drunk on alcohol and her grief. I rubbed the

sleep from my eyes and could, without the help of my glasses, determine

that it was a little after midnight. Jake and Josh were in tow as she

berated me for my lack of sympathy.

The episode ended with me crying, backed into a corner as she

screamed drunken insults at me while Josh and Jake held her back. I

didn't fail to notice that Easton didn't take up for me or try to step in to

protect me. They finally got her to calm down, and I tried (and failed

miserably, I might add) to go back to sleep.

It was evident that it was time to make my escape. There I was

again, seemingly nowhere to go, and I was running from the situation.

The next day, Easton and I drove around to find a homeless shelter or

church to take us both in, but none would since we weren't yet

married. We eventually gave up trying. Easton had been speaking with his mom throughout the day via text, and when we returned to Tessa's, she apologized for scaring me but insisted she didn't remember it. I apologized for not supporting her. I questioned how she could be genuinely apologetic if she couldn't remember what she'd done. She didn't seem sorry, not really. I found out later that Easton had made her apologize to keep the peace.

A couple of months later, I chose to spend Thanksgiving with Mom in an attempt to reconcile and because I hadn't quite gotten over how Tessa had treated me. No matter what life threw at me, I believed I should always be able to count on my mom, if she were willing to have me. Easton followed me to Mom's, much to Tessa's dismay.

To be fair, he knew that my anxiety would all but drive me crazy if we were away from each other. The thoughts in my head of him being with or texting other girls would race until they were completely out of control, and I would end up accusing him of doing things just because they'd crossed my mind. He couldn't reason with me. It was easier to just go along with me than fight my fears.

Mom would spend the holiday with her neighbors in the apartment below hers. After we'd eaten and returned to Tessa's, I lay down for a nap, as Easton and I had planned to try out Black Friday shopping for the first time that night. To be honest, I didn't want to spend the holiday around a group of people whose inhibitions were lowered by alcohol consumption, and I assumed, based on what I thought Tessa had told them about me, that they didn't care for me. I didn't want to put myself in a situation where they could verbally attack me again.

After our nap, we set off into the wild experience of shopping for Black Friday in America, passing a tipsy Tessa and Jake sitting on the living room couch. Tessa said she was surprised we weren't spending the holiday with her. I could tell she was hurt, but I didn't care. She'd hurt me, and I'd been hurt so much by everyone around me that I couldn't bring myself to see past my pain to care about hers.

While we were out, she must have continued to drink because she released her vengeance on me via text message. She started innocently, telling me how disappointed she was that we hadn't spent Thanksgiving with her. I lashed out at her, lacking self-control, empathy, and maturity. I blamed her and refused to take responsibility for my part – like how I usually made Easton feel guilty for not spending all his time with me because I was too insecure to have him be away from me. I was worried he'd find something better or forget about me. Even though I hadn't come out and asked him to spend the day with me, Easton responded like it was an unwritten rule or expectation. He knew the wrath he would face from me otherwise. I was not easy to love. I wouldn't admit to that because I didn't see it. All I saw was how everyone else around me was in the wrong.

She kicked me out that night via text while I stood in the middle of Target, shopping for Christmas gifts for our families. We spent that night at Abigail's house, as they were out of town for Thanksgiving and needed someone to operate their wood-burning stove so their pipes didn't freeze. In the following days, we made a game plan, fumbling through the darkness of where life had taken us. Easton, only seventeen years old then, decided to leave with me rather than stand up to his mom and fight this.

After the Thanksgiving break, Easton and I stayed with Mom for a couple of months while we figured out where we would end up. All the while, Tessa blamed me. She'd send long paragraphs to Easton, blaming me for stealing him away. I'd never asked him to come with me, though he still felt he had to in order to make me happy.

I was desperate for him to notice me, convinced that he was thinking of someone else if he wasn't thinking of and focused on me. He had grown up having his mother do everything for him, and now he followed me mindlessly. I wasn't worthy of the leadership role. We eventually moved into an apartment, got a dog, and tried our best to leave all the negativity behind.

Like my mother, I was full of hope and good intentions. My trauma had inhibited me from trusting anyone else's judgment and decisions, so I unquestioningly and wrongfully trusted only my own. I wasn't well-versed enough to be calling the shots, but I'd grown tired of being let down by everyone else. I didn't feel like they were acting in my best interest.

Easton was a moth, desperate for someone to take care of him, and I was the toxic flame he flew to. Looking back, I realize how strange our dynamic was - I was acting as his mother, trying to keep his selfish and impulsive tendencies in line while he, like a pubescent boy, snuck around and did what he wanted anyway.

Easton rarely listened to me and instead told me whatever he felt he needed to to get me to leave him alone before he did what he wanted anyway. There was no regard for our relationship, and my trust and respect in him continued to dwindle.

I hung on, hoping beyond hope that our relationship would get better and that Easton would magically change. I was bitter at the unfairness of it all. I was the older of the two of us, so most of the decision-making also rested on my shoulders, whether I wanted it to or not. I'd convinced myself and everyone around me that I was trustworthy regarding big decisions because I equated my experience with maturity. I'd been through so much. The two are not interchangeable, though, and my sense of judgment was deeply skewed. I hadn't had many good examples of what to do, and my trauma inhibited me from being able to make sound decisions – I was still in fight-or-flight mode, as I'd been my whole life. I'd cut off Easton's family completely, as I'd done so many times with Stella and my mother. Once I felt someone had wronged me, it was easier for me to just not be in contact with the people who'd hurt me. They'd lost their chance and had proven their untrustworthiness, so they had nothing more to offer me. I was very unforgiving toward people and their wrongdoings. It was a trauma response; It was a survival mechanism.

A few months before we married, I made up with Tessa and reconciled with his family, much to their chagrin. Easton had been visiting his grandfather – Tessa's dad – as his health was declining, and he was exhibiting signs of dementia. Tessa had stopped by while we were there – I'd done my best up to this point to avoid her as much as possible. Taking that as our cue to leave, I hugged Easton's Grandpa Timmy as Tessa walked into the bedroom. Timmy asked why I wouldn't hug Tessa as I got up to leave. I hesitated before I wrapped my arms around her. Our bodies shook with the sobs that were heavy with hurt and blame as we held each other.

She and I briefly talked in the dining room, and I realized Tessa had blamed me for Easton failing high school. She'd had this idea that I was a siren who'd dragged away her son and forced him to drop out of high school. She wouldn't listen to reason or accept that Easton's laziness caused him to fail high school. Rather than admit that her permissive parenting style had caused Easton's lack of personal responsibility, I was the scapegoat for blame. Again. Either way, she accepted me back into her life, and Easton and I moved forward with planning our wedding now that we had his family's "blessing." I spent hours pinning ideas on Pinterest and planning each detail and decoration.

I put together every decoration independently and insisted that everything be perfect. My fingers were often bloody and calloused from the abuse of the hot glue gun. I believed that a perfect wedding would then, naturally, lead to an ideal marriage. My goal was perfection, and I about killed myself trying to do both for our wedding and marriage.

Wedding days are supposed to be the stuff of fairy tales – they're what little girls dream and fantasize about. If our wedding day could have been any indication of how our marriage would be, I would have gathered the train of my wedding dress in my hands and run far, far away. We got married in September – exactly three years to the day after we started dating – and the heat was suffocating. On the day of, I had to finish decorating instead of getting ready for a wedding, and my stress levels were high, as one can imagine.

The DJ canceled on us at the last second, and we scrambled to find a replacement. Easton's brother had done some hard drugs, and he was unable to function. Easton's extended family had come in from New York. They were the fun ones – the first ones on the dance floor at any event. There was no fun to be had at our wedding. I already had a feeling that they didn't like me and blamed me for stealing Easton, and this was all the confirmation I needed – again, I filtered the experience through my skewed lens.

Sweat poured off of me all day, and I was so frustrated by the end that I ended the reception an hour early because I just wanted to go home and get away from everyone.

Still in our wedding attire, Easton and I swung through a Wendy's drive-thru on our way home for food since we hadn't had time to eat much at the reception. We sat in the living room of our apartment, eating chicken nuggets and fries, and for the first time that day, I felt relaxed.

That spring, during my last semester of college, Easton lost the best job he ever had. He was working at a local car engine manufacturing plant. The job offered excellent benefits and pay and would have set him up for life. During the year-long probation period, the temporary worker works the night shift.

With only a couple of days left in his probation period, Easton and I were excited about his upcoming promotion, which would enable him to get hired full-time, get a pay raise, and help him get more regular work hours. The only downside was the lack of time we spent together because of the opposite shifts, as my student teaching took place during regular work hours.

Easton had lost so many jobs before this that I'd stopped expecting him to be able to provide for me – it was evident that the responsibility rested solely on my shoulders. We hadn't developed a healthy relationship with healthy boundaries and parameters, nor did we trust or respect each other. So, when Easton came home earlier than usual, crying and begging me to forgive him for losing his job, I was immediately suspicious of his story. He'd already lied to my face so much that I wasn't inclined to believe him.

A few months later, after I'd officially graduated with my degree in education, I landed a job at a high school within our district with a reputation that preceded it. The students had a reputation for causing problems and being challenging to manage.

I'd chosen to complete my student-teaching hours there as I convinced myself that if I could survive teaching students like these, anywhere else would be a breeze. I went into it scared out of my wits of what was to come.

I expected the students to yell at me, curse me, and berate me for my teaching abilities, or lack thereof. Instead, I was met with eager students who hung on to my every word and those who opened up to me about their rough lives at home. I fell in love with the students and my ability to connect and empathize with them. Pain is an adhesive, and I was stuck like glue.

Chapter Twenty-Two: I Couldn't Make This Up if I Tried

I was the stereotypical overzealous Pinterest-perfect teacher during my first year of teaching after I graduated college. I had binders for everything – different types of assessments (that I never gave), strategies for teaching (that I never looked at), and print-outs of attendance (that I never used because attendance was already digital by this point). I also had an organized binder for my 10th-grade students' information to have all their essential details - contact information, parent/guardian contact information, and class schedule in one place. Toward the end of the first semester, I cleaned out the binder, removing the papers of students who had transferred to another class or an alternative school.

I came across a familiar name on one of the student pages: Brandon was on the list as the father, with the same HVAC workplace listed that I had come to associate with him.

I hadn't noticed when I'd collected the paperwork and organized them in the binder, but things with work had finally slowed down enough that I wasn't in fight-or-flight mode. Everything inside me clenched up, tensing up to take on the brunt of the painful revelation: he was still choosing another kid over me. Not only that, but this kid, Lucas, was in my class. I felt like I was living out a soap opera or a *Lifetime* movie.

I knew I had to approach this situation delicately and that saying the wrong thing at the wrong time could prove disastrous. I was curious to unveil this situation's delicate layers while searching for the truth. I began asking innocent enough questions to test the waters. If Lucas happened to think highly of Brandon, I didn't want to be the one to spoil that for him, though it was a highly tempting thing to do.

I began by asking him if he and his dad got along. Lucas told me that his father was in prison.

"Well, who is that listed on your contact paper for this class?" I said with a furrowed brow.

"Oh, Brandon. He's my stepdad. Well, kind of. He's been with my mom for a few years now."

I tapped my chin as I absorbed the bit of information, and I left it at that for a few weeks. I didn't want to push the situation too much.

A few weeks later, I randomly asked at the end of class while we were all waiting for the bell to ring, "So, do you and your stepdad have a good relationship? Do you guys get along?" I was hopeful at this point. In my head, I imagined Brandon as this super-involved and encouraging dad who would play catch with me in the yard. Even if he couldn't be that for me, I wanted him to be that for someone else.

Lucas scoffed, "Uh, no. I hate him. We fight all the time," he said, with some added expletives.

"What do you mean?" I asked, my voice laced with worry.

"Like, we physically fight. I beat the [crap] out of Brandon when he gets drunk and tries to go after my mom." Lucas explained.

My heart sank. I don't know why I seemed to have a continuous supply of hope for this man. What a waste of hope and expectation. Even though there was no reason whatsoever to be surprised by this revelation that he was fighting with teenage boys - people smaller and weaker than him in stature - in his free time, I couldn't help but still be crushed. I wanted so badly for there to be some redeeming quality in him.

Toward the end of the school year, I told Lucas to ask Brandon how he knew Destinee Vance and then report back to me after the weekend. Again, Brandon had dug this hole himself. I wanted to see him get himself out of this one.

I also didn't think it was fair of me, Lucas's 10th-grade English teacher, to drop this bomb on him. It should come from someone who has known him longer - like Brandon.

While I waited to hear back, I gossiped with my co-workers in the hallways between classes, them over a cup of coffee and me over a bottle of water, each of us predicting how things would go. I was, as usual, a unique childhood tale among my peers. I loved to watch the horror and pity spread across their faces as I relayed the details of my trauma. Everyone always commented that no one would ever know I'd been through anything because I displayed such a happy demeanor. I was good at hiding it. The same was true for this situation.

I was good at hiding how much it bothered me that Brandon was willing to be an active part of someone else's life, especially knowing he missed out on every moment of mine. Even if it wasn't an enjoyable time, he was choosing to spend time with someone else's child, who could have been God's way of sending him a second chance.

I was still rooting for him to get it right, so at least I could feel like my missing out was worth something since it hadn't been for Hannah either. Brandon let me down yet again. You'd think I'd be used to it, but because he was my parent, I looked up to him to be a good role model and lead me.

The following Monday, after a long weekend of fretting over the response, Lucas approached me before the first period with an incredulous look.

"Well?" I asked, eager to hear his response.

"Well," Lucas said, leaning against the wall beside me, "at first, he said that you two used to date."

I wanted to sob loudly and laugh out loud at the same time.

"But I knew that couldn't be right, so I kept asking him." Lucas continued.

Thank God he knew better. The absolute nerve of that man to ever even consider the idea that I would ever in a million years want to degrade myself by being in a relationship with someone as loathsome as he was astonishing. How disgusting of him to even suggest that. I was his daughter, yet he showed how little he thought of me.

I was hanging onto every word, eager to see how my father - the other half who created me - viewed me and the value that he placed on me.

"Then he said you guys used to live together," Lucas explained. Again, the degradation of what and who I was to him was baffling, "but I knew that wasn't right either."

At least some in this situation had some sense. Oh, my goodness. I couldn't believe what I was hearing.

"Then he finally admitted that you were his daughter." And there it was—the bomb dropped. But somehow, the damage was nothing compared to the shock I'd already endured in the earlier jokes that were Brandon's responses to our relationship.

Brandon showed up at the Veterans' Day assembly the following November. Lucas was in JROTC at the school, and Brandon had been in the military for a brief time and came to be honored at the assembly. I knew it was him when I locked eyes with him across the gymnasium. Drinking had aged him badly – his hair was all white, his face was heavy with inflammation, and his beer belly stuck way out. I wanted to scream and cry and run away. He showed up for this kid, who's not even his, but he couldn't show up for me. Not once. Not even a little.

He saw me on the way out after the assembly concluded and approached me. I picked up my speed to avoid him because I knew I would lose my job for what I'd say to him if he approached me.

I wouldn't be able to hold my tongue anymore. So, I turned the other cheek and hurried away to avoid him.

I was too angry at him to face him and have him lie more about why he hadn't been in my life. I blamed him for not being there, convinced he could have stopped Mom if he had been in my life.

I created this fairytale in my head that we could have been a happy family had he stuck around. Mom would not have lost her mind again because he would have provided her stability.

Chapter Twenty-Three: Double-Duty

Even though I was unhappy in my marriage, I stayed because that's what you do. I had convinced myself this was just how life was, and this was love, even though it was wretched and self-serving on both accounts. I had come to accept that the love stories in my favorite Nicholas Sparks novels were just that - stories. I convinced myself that kind of love wasn't real and that most people were miserable in their marriages. I was so depressed, and that was not at all what I wanted in life. I felt like a shell of myself because I still hadn't developed a sense of identity. But this is what everyone wanted in life – this was the American Dream. Guilt dragged me into the abyss of depression again and again because I hated that I wasn't happy. The sense of unrest in my soul was maddening.

But that's not what I presented to those around me and on social media. No, I put on a front that everything was great and we were happy. I took the time to craft the most eloquently worded social media posts about Easton, bragging about our love at any chance I could.

I wanted people to think things were excellent and we were happy, wishing I was narrating the truth with every type of word. It was a continuation of the production, which was our wedding.

That's not to say that we didn't have fun times or enjoy each other's company because we did. But I was not a good wife to him. I didn't trust him, nor could I communicate effectively; I was verbally abusive toward him over simple issues. Still, I was so focused on Easton's shortcomings and downfalls that I couldn't see my major flaws and how I was damaging our marriage.

We bought a house toward the end of my first year of teaching. We were as hopeful as ever that moving would magically fix our problems with a simple change of location. We wrongfully believed that elevating ourselves in materialistic ways like this will magically fix our lives. We even started attending a new local church, hoping to start anew and find God. But we also weren't willing to let go of our vices and focus on God so He could work in us.

He'd gotten a job washing and detailing cars for Enterprise, which was hard manual labor. Because of his depression, though, he didn't bother to put in any effort when it came to personal hygiene. I constantly reminded him to brush his teeth or shower, and he often came home from work reeking of body odor.

He would eat an entire bag of Doritos for dinner when he didn't want chicken and fries or Ramen noodles, and I followed suit to try to make him happy. We were both miserable, and neither had the gumption to pull the other out of the trenches.

Easton and I did what most struggling couples do in an attempt to fix their marriage: we started trying for a baby. Mostly, it was because his brother and his brother's girlfriend had recently gotten pregnant. I was furious when I found out! I had done everything right according to society's rules - gotten married, bought a house, waited to have kids - and I expected to have favor with both sides of Easton's family. But Josh and his girlfriend would be welcoming Tessa and Jake's first grandchild, which would, from my perspective, automatically win them favor over us. It didn't matter that they weren't married or that neither of them had a decent-paying job, a college education, or a house, which I believed were prerequisites to having a baby and raising a family. I felt they were being rewarded for their failures and shortcomings, and I could not handle it.

I was so cruel to Josh's pregnant girlfriend, and I hated her for being doted upon and accepted by the family for breaking tradition. I hated her for everything that I wasn't, and I made her pregnancy miserable. I couldn't even stand for her to talk about her pregnancy around me. What was supposed to be one of the happiest times of her life was ruined because of my insecurities.

One day, the summer after we moved into our house, I dropped Easton off at work, promptly drove home, and went back to sleep. When I woke up, I rolled over onto my back in bed and opened my eyes. I looked up at the ceiling, and everything twisted back and forth like a DJ scratching a record. I stumbled out of bed, crawled up the stairs, and went straight to the bathroom, promptly ripping open the plastic packaging of the home pregnancy test and praying for good news.

Without looking because I didn't want to get my hopes up again, I placed the test on the sink, waiting for the results to show. Something in my being felt different, so I wasn't surprised when I looked at the test and found the two pink lines. And I've never been more thankful for something so simple in my entire life. Even though I wasn't surprised by this gift of a response, that didn't dampen my level of thankfulness. I hit my knees and thanked God for this tremendous blessing to someone as undeserving as me.

I immediately loved the little life form growing inside of me. My resentment toward Brandon deepened because I couldn't imagine not loving this little life - who was only the size of a poppy seed at that point - despite any conditions that may come our way.

How could he, knowing what it's like to have a child already and having been through that, still walk away? I lay down on the couch, tears streaming down my face, placed my hands on my stomach, and prayed that God would protect my baby from the things that I had endured. I prayed that He would help me be a better mother, and I promised my baby that I would never leave. I had decided that it would take nothing short of an act of God to keep me away from my baby. My heart hurt at even the thought.

Meanwhile, I was terrified that my pregnancy was just a dream because it was too good to be true. The old familiar fears of being just like my mother crept back in, and I fought off the belief that I was going to hurt this precious baby. I couldn't imagine it. I was also terrified of not being able to protect my precious baby since it was apparent nobody had protected me.

While I secretly hoped for a girl since I was so into make-up, frills, glitter, and lace, I wasn't disappointed when God blessed me with a boy. I somehow knew He would because of the deep need for me to experience the all-consuming love of a boy, and what better way than by the unconditional love of a son?

So, when, in the ultrasound room with his parents and grandmother and my mother on the sofa, the ultrasound tech told us we were having a little boy, my heart swelled with excitement.

I so enjoyed being pregnant, especially during the holiday season. I ate all the things with no shame whatsoever, claiming that the baby necessitated it. I developed an unhealthy relationship with food and saw it as a way to fill the voids in my life. The day I went in to give birth to our son, I weighed in at two hundred pounds, and only 7 pounds and 7 ounces of that was baby.

Though I thought my body was going to burst from the pain of childbirth, my focus shifted from the pain to my precious baby boy in my arms as soon as I laid eyes on him. He was the most beautiful thing I'd ever seen, so wrinkly and innocent. And I looked down at him, and my heart swelled with a more intense love than I'd ever known. I'd never felt real love like that, and it overwhelmed me so much that I couldn't help but weep, mainly because I felt so undeserving of this love. Then my little boy, whose skin was so incredibly soft and smooth against my own, lifted his little head, bobbing from the effort the whole time, and looked me right in the eyes as if to reassure me that I did. I wept.

We named him Sawyer mainly because it was such a strong name. He was the most perfect little human I'd ever seen. And I couldn't believe he was all mine. That night, after I'd been sewn up and had given up caring about the busted blood vessels on my forehead from pushing so hard, reality set in.

Sure, I'd helped Stella care for her little boys for years - fed them, changed diapers, bathed them, and laid them down for bed- but I didn't trust myself as a mother; I had no idea what I was doing. Not on my own. I'd changed Sawyer's diaper that night after a failed feeding – he wasn't latching correctly. When I laid him back down in the clear plastic bassinet, he started aspirating on his spit-up. It was silent, and I wouldn't have known had I not been standing above him to see it. I hit the emergency call button on my bed, scooped him up into my arms, and sat him up so he could breathe again. The nurse came in, breathless and expecting a more chaotic scene.

"He was choking on his spit up," I explained, shaking as reality set in. Sawyer could have choked and died. It was that easy.

'That happens," she said calmly but annoyed at being called in for nothing. She placed her hands into her scrub pockets.

"But what if it happens and I'm asleep and not there to save him?" I spat out, desperate to calm the vivid and morbid scenarios shuttering through my brain at the time.

"Your mommy instincts will alert you, and you'll wake up," she said too casually, as if life didn't hang in the balance here.

"And what if they don't?" I asked, desperate for an answer to ease my fears.

She stopped straightening the room, looked at me, and said, "Then, I don't know."

My heart dropped. What if I was so heavily asleep that Sawyer choked on his spit, and I wasn't there to save him? How could I protect him? The thought of Sawyer dying drove me mad, and my mind refused to shut off long enough to allow me to sleep. My anxiety kept me awake the entire time we were in the hospital.

By the time we got home three days later, I was an exhausted shell of a human. My processing speed was that of dial-up Internet. I walked around the house, trying to get housework done, but never getting further than one step before I got distracted by something else that needed doing. I remember regretting having Sawyer, not because I didn't love him, but because I loved him so much that I couldn't bear the thought of anything or anyone hurting him. I felt ill-equipped to protect him against all the world's dangers and keep his innocence from being ripped away. I realize now that even my hypervigilance, which I still struggle to rein in to this day, is a trauma response to my not being protected by those who were supposed to protect me at all costs.

Meanwhile, I would stop and stare at Sawyer and just weep at how precious and perfect he was. The chubbiness of his cheeks, the length of his eyelashes, his little tufts of hair, and the pout of his lips brought tears to my eyes.

How had someone as damaged and broken as me created something so incredibly perfect? It made me feel so inadequate. I had done nothing good to deserve such a perfect little human as the one staring and cooing back at me.

With my walls down, I had this sinking feeling in my chest. I knew I was still too broken ever to give this beautiful little boy all the love that he deserved. I also knew that there was no way that I would ever be deserving of the love that this perfect little angel had already gracefully bestowed upon me. The weight of this realization pushed me further into post-partum depression.

It didn't help that Easton, who had been ultra-reliant on his mother growing up, was now ultra-reliant on me. I don't think I ever paid attention to it until Sawyer was born and I realized I was taking on the brunt of the household responsibilities. I didn't mind caring for Sawyer – that was my job as his mother.

I enjoyed it and relished that I was entrusted to care for him like only a mother can. However, I did not enjoy continuing to care for a grown man. The more I stepped up to take on his shirking responsibilities, the less Easton did.

Tasks needed to be done either way, and it was not worth it to fight with him about it. I silently – and begrudgingly – did them on my own to keep our household functioning.

As the responsibilities piled on me, the weight of the stress did, too. Before I realized it, I was drowning again. I brought up the discrepancies to Easton, hoping that my bringing it to his attention would help him realize his shortcomings. Granted, again, I wasn't that great of a communicator, but he was patient and listened to me.

Things were better for a couple of weeks – he would step up and help care for Sawyer or clean without me constantly reminding him or making him a list of simple tasks to complete, such as taking out the garbage. Then he would slack off again, and the responsibilities were back on me to keep the household running. I'd quietly bear the weight of the obligations for a few months until I couldn't take it anymore. This cycle repeated itself for over a year. I felt like I was pouring my heart and soul into providing for my family in every way, but nobody was refilling my cup. It's impossible to pour from an empty cup; mine was bone dry.

Chapter Twenty-Four: Running is What I Do Best

I'd gotten too comfortable in my misery and brokenness, and though I quickly took on the role of caretaker, it was a role that became overwhelming because I had little to no help. Don't get me wrong, Easton was and still is a good guy – he's got a good heart and benign intentions. There's no drive to be better, though. He's content on staying where and how he is without considering how his stagnation drags down those around him. I tried being a good role model by bettering myself – pursuing my master's degree or working out and eating healthier to lose weight to inspire him to do the same. I was met with the same resolute contentment as before.

Resentment started to grow in the pit of my stomach as the realization that our family's livelihood rested solely on my shoulders settled down on me. As the resentment grew, my respect for him lessened. This is not the life I envisioned for myself – I was supposed to be taken care of, not taking care of everything and everyone around me. So, I did what I did best when things got challenging for me. Rather than face and live with my choice to marry him and start a family with Easton, I ran.

During our almost five-year marriage, I constantly fell in and out of love/infatuation with his friends and other boys around me. I coveted being cared for the way they seemed capable of doing; I had convinced myself that the grass was greener in someone else's pasture. That's when I realized I'd garnered the attention of the technology specialist at work, whose office was right across the hall from my classroom. The two of us, Jason and me, quickly struck up an affair, and I hid my offense from Easton for a few weeks.

While it was still a physical affair, it was primarily emotional, as he understood my trauma much more profoundly than any man ever had before him. I had finally found someone who listened to me and could connect with me on a deep, emotional level like I'd never experienced before.

For the first time in my life, I felt seen. He was able to understand my pain and empathize with me. He didn't take and take from me like Easton had. He offered to help me and support me as much as he could. He was able to help me put the pieces of the puzzle that was my life together and for the first time, the whole mess started to make a little more sense.

Through him, I was starting to become aware of the matted mess of emotional turmoil I'd experienced during my lifetime and how it was affecting my behaviors up until this point. I'd just gone through life without acknowledging how incredibly broken I was as I'd been too busy taking care of everyone else – Stella's kids and then Easton. But Jason didn't need to be taken care of; he saw my brokenness and provided a space for me to heal.

I admitted to my transgressions when Easton confronted me one evening about his suspicions. After dealing with Easton's lies throughout the years, I was willing to own up to my mistakes because I didn't want to hurt him by lying like he'd done to me so often. But I wasn't willing to give up the affair.

I'd spent my whole life with my eyes tightly shut to the emotional storms and mental anguish inside of me, convinced that there was no hope for me. I'd finally gotten my first taste of hope and couldn't let that go.

Easton was hurt. I'd blindsided him and betrayed his trust seemingly without provocation or warning. He gave me the ultimatum: end the affair or end our marriage. I felt alive with Jason; he was willing and able to care for me, so I chose him.

I wish I could tell you that Jason and I ran off into the sunset together and lived happily ever after, but that is far from true. Our extra-marital affair and pre-marital sex had set us up to fail from the get-go.

It didn't help that I was in a made-up internal competition with all the girls Jason had been with before me, and it drove me insane. I became obsessed with looking physically better than all of them – even though I had no idea what they looked like, save his ex-wife. The only thing I knew about her was that she was super skinny when they were together. So, I aimed for that.

I had gained so much weight during my pregnancy, using it as an excuse to binge eat my negative emotions. When I finally started to focus on my fitness, I quickly became obsessed, and developed an eating disorder. I counted every single calorie and tracked my intake. If I went over my allotted calories, I either made myself throw up or ran it off at the gym. I got down to 114 pounds with 20 percent body fat. I still thought I was fat and that I needed to lose weight, never mind the fact that I could see my ribs and I had a six-pack.

I thought I was ugly, so I scheduled procedures like Botox and other procedures to remove and reduce fat on my body. I convinced myself that if I didn't look perfect, Jason would leave me for someone better, just like I'd convinced myself Brandon had done.

The guilt of my decision to split up my family I'd fought so hard to build weighed heavily on me. I got phone calls and texts from Easton's family and mine, begging us to work it out. I refused to budge.

For the first time in years, my eyes were wide open to the potential within myself because I had someone pushing me to improve instead of it all being on me. Then COVID-19 shut down the whole world, and I had nothing but time to think about what I'd done and to get to know Jason. He moved in with me since I couldn't afford to pay the bills alone. We both came with emotional baggage, and I was learning things about his past that I didn't like. These are things that made me jealous and insecure, and they exposed all of my flaws and shortcomings.

I missed Easton and his familiarity - the safety that came with knowing he wouldn't go anywhere, no matter how much I pushed. He enjoyed a nice, cushy life while I cared for him. I wasn't in love with him, but I was in love with the idea of him and the idea of what he represented. I was in love with the hope that I had for our future. Easton saw the ugliest parts of me and stayed.

I don't think it was out of love, but instead out of not wanting to give up the familiar. I mourned the familiar life with Easton that I'd lost. I mourned his family, as I'd lost them too.

I mourned my reputation, as I knew he was going around telling everyone who would listen that his wife cheated on him to make himself look like the victim. Nobody knew my side of the story. Nobody bothered to ask, and I didn't bother to tell anybody. Still, that was a hard pill to swallow: the utter desolation of one's reputation. Especially since it was a façade, I'd worked so hard to cultivate. As it's been proven just through my family's stories, though, whatever is behind the closed doors of the façade will eventually leak out. I had held everything in for so long, all the hurt that had built up over my lifetime. I'd never allowed myself to mourn or meditate on anything. But the hurt was now so intense that it spilled over, and I could no longer keep it in. I felt like such a failure. I should have just stuck out the miserable marriage for Sawyer. I struggled to stay alive that summer as I contemplated suicide more times than I can count. I finally had space to hurt, and I was in agony.

I leaned on Mom during my divorce from Easton because I didn't know who else to turn to. Moms are supposed to be someone you can count on to love you no matter what.

Even though she had proven time and again that her love was, in fact, conditional, she helped carry me emotionally that year. She was the one who could understand my situation the most, and I figured she would be the least judgmental. Mom and I had many long phone conversations about my complaints and I poured my heart out to her. She shared many of her life stories with me during this time, though there was a lot I still didn't know.

She became my rock. I knew I was letting Stella down, but I was too ashamed to reach out to her. I assumed she'd judge me and tell me

How disappointing I was. I didn't need that – I carried enough disappointment for the both of us – I needed grace.

Jason and I fought constantly. The juxtaposition of who I was and what I wanted the world to see was not so different from the façade my family had presented in the past. As much as I was trying to outrun the truth and prove that I was better, my refusal to face reality kept me rooted in the mess. I'd been able to primarily manipulate Easton because he'd learned to follow both his mother and then me unthinkingly, but Jason was not to be fooled. He called me out on my manipulation, which led me to get defensive and lash out because I didn't like what I saw. He saw me for who I was – the broken mess – and for what I could be.

I fought him at every turn, still refusing to accept that I was the problem. My inability to take responsibility for anything that I'd done wrong came from seeing myself as emotionally marred beyond repair. I knew I was a piece of garbage, but I couldn't accept that others saw me like that, too, especially when I tried so hard to please everyone and make everyone like me. I didn't like myself, but I needed somebody to.

Additionally, he was so battered by women during his lifetime that he took my venting and emotional instability personally – like it was directed at him. Even though he had caused this, he still felt like he was being blamed for it. I didn't have the communication skills to explain that it was just a build of past pain leaking out, and he didn't

have the communication skills to realize that it was not about him.

Unfortunately, his two kids, whom he shared with his ex-wife,

were there to witness most of it. I blamed them for causing problems

when it was my insecurities. I couldn't accept the blame because, again,

I'd already felt like I was damaged and flawed enough. I told myself that

if Jason saw any more ugliness in me, he would leave.

Chapter Twenty-Five: Healing Isn't Pretty

Mom had been on medication to balance out her moods and emotions for her whole life. The doctors had recently discovered that a drug that Mom had been taking for decades to even out her chemical imbalances was severely damaging her heart. They were unable to find a medication to provide the same level of tranquility since. The doctors continued to offer her various medicines in hopes of finding something to work. Still, nobody had ever wanted to help her get to the bottom of her pain to understand it and heal. She carried it around with her still. It was heavy and etched in the intimations of her physical well-being, or lack thereof. She was diabetic, had high blood pressure, heart problems, tremors, migraines, insomnia, and sleep apnea, among other physical ailments. All of which were physical manifestations of the trauma she'd endured and the havoc that it had wreaked on her emotional and mental well-being.

She had kicked John out of the government-funded apartment they shared years before because he was on pills and was allowing random people to stop by. The two were still in love, and Mom still did everything she could to support John in his separate dwelling, despite his spiraling drug addiction. She went to the store for him and drove him to many appointments. He'd had his license revoked years prior for too many DUIs. The chemical imbalances, along with the stress of COVID shutting everything down and John's drug use, had caused Mom's manic and depressive episodes to get worse. The more stressful life got for her, the further the pendulum swung to either side of the spectrum; thus, the more intense her emotions and episodes were.

Mom called me one snowy day, wanting me to look at some lawyer paperwork – it was of no alarm. I told her I couldn't make it out that day because the roads were icy, and I didn't want to risk it. She took personal offense to my telling her no, told me she didn't love me, and told me I was selfish before she hung up. Her radio silence didn't last long, though. She left me strings of voicemails for weeks at a time after that, each one cussing me out worse than the last time. I learned just to ignore her calls.

John was eventually admitted to the hospital after having a stroke, and the doctors discovered a concoction of drugs in his system including meth and heroin.

Mom was dumbfounded and felt betrayed that he could be doing drugs like this when he was supposed to love and support her like she was him. Nevertheless, Mom catered to his every need while he was in the hospital, even standing outside his window in a mask so that she could see him.

He died that April, and Mom lost her sense of purpose. Mom had built her life around caring for John for the past few years. She lost the person who'd stuck with her through it all. They'd had a toxic relationship from the start, but they had gotten addicted to that toxicity. Somewhere along the way, they mistook the toxicity for love and the fighting for passion and built their relationship on that foundation. I don't think they ever really loved each other, as I've come to understand love to be. They tried their best with what they were given, which was enough for both of them.

Mom fell apart after John died. Anytime she felt shortness of breath, even sitting in her living room, she'd call for an ambulance to get her. Never mind that she had an oxygen tank in her bedroom for such purposes. Once the doctors released Mom from the hospital, or she decided she no longer wanted to be there, she'd start making calls for people to come get her. Most of the time, it was in the middle of the night. When I explained to her that I had to get up with Sawyer in a few hours or be at work soon, she'd berate me for letting her down.

I learned to set my phone to Do Not Disturb to get some semi-decent sleep before work the next day. She'd get mad at whoever refused or ignored her calls, leading to her leaving mean voicemails for weeks until she calmed down. I'd stopped answering her phone calls and even stopped listening to her voicemails, choosing instead just to delete them rather than listen to how much she hated me. I was desperately searching for peace in my life, and the drama she brought was too much for me to handle.

Meanwhile, I was still starving myself and feeling more and more inadequate as the days went on. The only way I knew how to improve myself and prove myself to Jason was physically, so I pushed myself at the gym. I was still a mental and emotional wreck, but at least my body looked better than it ever had.

It was an endless cycle, and I couldn't drag myself off the hamster wheel. I was so obviously stuck in fight-or-flight in desperate attempts to make everything look like it was perfect.

I felt like everything was out of control, and I felt out of control. I constantly accused Jason of things I assumed he was doing. When he denied doing anything, I refused to believe him. Easton had lied to me so much, and Brandon had given me nothing but excuses, that I'd come to see all men as liars. I was miserable and hurting, feeling more and more worthless with each passing day.

I yelled at Jason, cussed at him, kicked him out of the house, and then begged him to come back. His kids saw it all, but I didn't care; I was too focused on my own pain. I was too focused on feeling unloved to stop and realize how I made them feel. But I did everything possible to ensure Sawyer felt unique and protected. I took him out on fun outings, and Jason's kids, too, if they were there that weekend. I made sure to plaster the photos all over social media so people could see how great of a mom I was.

To be fair, I was trying to work through my trauma and baggage. There was so much of it, though, that I didn't even know where to start. It was overwhelming.

Jason left for the first time after I slapped him across the face. We'd just celebrated Sawyer's third birthday, and as usual, I had gone above and beyond in decorating and ensuring everything looked perfect. The stress had gotten to me, as I felt the pressure of the need to be perfect weighing me down.

We'd gotten into a heated argument about something I can't recall now, and Jason left that night, unable to handle my craziness anymore. The little bit that I could hold together just fell apart. I didn't eat for almost a week straight. My heart physically hurt and felt like it was going to break right in half.

Jason had promised me he wouldn't leave, yet he was proving to be like everyone else. I felt so betrayed. I could have choked on the emotional pain.

I immediately went on a desperate search for love in all the wrong places, setting up a dating profile on Facebook. I garnered immediate attention, but nothing could touch the pain I felt. All I wanted was Jason. He, too, knew what it was like to hurt. He tried to help me, but I was drowning. I was too far gone. I wanted to be saved, but I didn't want to go through the healing process because I was comfortable in the darkness.

So again, I found myself praying for God to take my life in the middle of the night. I sat in my car in the garage with the engine running and the door closed. I understood precisely why Mom had done what she had done all those years ago. Not that I ever would have harmed Sawyer, but I felt that same sense of desperation and hopelessness. Just as my head started to nod as I approached the precipice of death, I opened the garage and saved myself.

I felt like Sawyer would be better off without me. I felt like he deserved better. I felt like, no matter how hard I tried, I could never protect him from dangers and trauma. I felt hopeless. I felt like I was a waste of God's creation. All I did was ruin people's lives. I was hurting, and I couldn't stop myself from breaking.

I was hurting others in the process, but I couldn't stop it either. I couldn't understand what it was all for. I was so incredibly tired of fighting for my life every single day. I just wanted a break, one that could only be found, I thought, in death. I begged for death - for peace.

Jason and I continued to talk and hang out during the separation, as we were drawn to each other. I'll never know whether destiny kept us tethered, but Jason and I reconciled just two weeks later. The break-up had been a wake-up call and led me to realize that things needed to change - I needed to change. We went into the relationship this time with renewed vision and understanding. Jason's perception of me was significantly damaged nonetheless. Jason had his trauma to deal with. He grew up in a verbally abusive household with his mother and was never taught how to communicate effectively.

Jason was the baby of the family, so his mom spoiled him a bit and would let him out of a chore now and then while his siblings still had to work. She got him into video games with the Super Nintendo, and then he used it to escape. When he got older, she got meaner. His mom controlled his every move, constantly told him "no", and yelled at him. She claimed to be a Christian, and sometimes, on Easter or Christmas, she had them read a verse from the Bible, but she was not living a Christian example.

Jason and his siblings were never allowed to trick-or-treat or dress up for Halloween because their mom said that it was devil worship. They would sneak to the living room window and peek behind the curtains to see the neighborhood kids dressed up for Halloween. If their mom caught them, she would chastise them and curse at them for participating.

She would also make proclamations when called out on her hypocrisy that she was a "G-D Christian". Jason eventually lost respect for his mom, and he began to resent Christians based on the example that was set for him.

Events such as these occurred with the future women in Jason's life, such as the emotional and mental abuse he endured under the spell of his ex-wife, whom he married twice in hopes of working things out for their two kids.

Neither time did she do anything to mediate Jason's view of women. She only added fuel to the fire, which helped further tip the scale, leaving Jason feeling both scared and hopeless when it came to meaningful relationships with women. These events strongly influenced a pretty negative perspective of women and inhibited him from respecting women as a whole.

My craziness and instability didn't help matters at all. We made compromises, ensuring we wouldn't cross each other's' boundaries anymore. Jason threatened to leave multiple times when it happened, even after he promised me he wouldn't.

I realized there was not much worth staying for, but I guilted him into staying—numerous times. The early years were plagued with miscommunication and fighting because of the lack of communication. Like my mother before me, I confused fighting with passion and lust with love.

After he left the first time, I realized that I could not trust him. That was the one thing Easton had never done - not until I had wholly driven him out - was leave me. No matter how bad things got between us, Easton always stayed. But Jason was secure enough in himself to realize that he didn't need to put up with my crap, so he left with confidence.

He looked me in the eyes and told me he didn't love me, but I could tell by looking at him that he did. I could see it in his eyes. We were both trying so hard to love one another. Neither of us had been shown good examples of love, so we fumbled in the dark. When he returned and we started our relationship anew, we started talking about getting engaged - something that had been entirely off the plate for him.

This gave me hope that things would continue to change for us. We drove to Calhoun County Park to look at the stars one warm evening in July. We'd grabbed some pizza and ice cream from a local brick oven pizzeria. The forecast predicted that the sky would be clear enough for us to see the stars, as we'd done many times before. But when we got to the top of the hill, we were bummed to see the sky was full of clouds. We spread out our blanket, and I laid down on my back with my arms behind my head, staring up at the stars, which were quickly becoming visible. It was as if God Himself had just blown away the clouds like He was blowing out candles. My view was completely unencumbered by any other light pollution or anything. I wept then, just like I did every time I caught a glimpse of the awesomeness of God. The sky was sprinkled with glittering stars, and I felt a sense of peace wash over me.

Just then, Jason asked me to locate my favorite constellation, Orion, which I did quickly and without hesitation. When I turned around, he was on one knee with the most beautiful diamond ring I'd ever seen, cushioned in a velvet box.

"Will you marry me?" he asked. I wrapped my arms around him, kissed him, and agreed that yes, I would. He scooped me up in his arms, and we cried together.

I didn't share the good news with anyone for a long time, not even Stella. She still did not like Jason and was rude and standoffish whenever she interacted with him. She reasoned that he knew that I was married, and yet he still chose to be a homewrecker and play a part in ruining my marriage. Though I saw her point of view, I wished she'd extended he and I some grace.

I answered Mom's call one day that summer after months of ignoring her and the drama she consistently brought on herself and those around her. She sobbed to me about how miserable she was and how desperate she was for Jesus to call her home. She sobbed to me about how scared she was of her neighbor at the apartment complex who had invited her up to dinner. She didn't accept the invitation because her paranoia had led her to believe that he was going to drug her. I learned that Mom had spent all her money going to yard sales that summer, so her the power company had shut off her utilities. Gertie and Dale paid to have it turned back on. When it didn't happen fast enough to Mom's liking, she called and cussed them out, too.

I learned that Mom had given Stella, Abigail, and Mamaw Goldie the same run-around. Yet she couldn't understand why people hesitated to talk to her. She couldn't see that she was the problem.

While I understood she was angry and upset about things in life, I tried to explain that that was no excuse to hurt the people she loved.

She broke down crying. "I just can't help it," she said, "I just get so mad."

"I understand, Mom," I said, "but you've got to learn to control yourself. Your words hurt people." I should have taken my advice at the time.

She got mad at me and cussed me out again toward the end of that call, saying that I was being insensitive to her because I kept calling her out. I was tired of her walking all over everybody and expecting them to come at her beck and call whenever she needed us. I still didn't know much about love, but I knew enough to recognize that that wasn't it.

She continued to call multiple times a week, and I just let the phone ring. Sometimes, I would listen to the voicemails until I came across a mean one. I'd stop listening to the voicemails, just deleting them instead of playing them, until I built up the courage to listen. Some were nice enough. She would just talk to me about her day like I had answered. Her back problems seemed to be getting worse, as she described finding it hard to get out of her car and walk up the sidewalk to her apartment. I felt badly for her, but I had been stung too many times to fall for it again and let her in. I was trying so hard to find peace that I couldn't be bothered by her drama. I stonewalled her.

Chapter Twenty-Six: Crippling Heartache

On October 22, 2021, I was driving to work separately from Jason, which was usual on Fridays. After we got off work, Jason had to drive an hour and a half away (one-way) to pick his kids up for the weekend, and I usually just preferred to go straight home after a long week of teaching. That morning, we would quickly stop at the local health department to get our COVID-19 vaccines.

Chelsea called me when I pulled off the exit, trying to focus on the road and remember the way to go. We were busy moms now - she was a recent mother of two. We'd resorted to messaging each other back and forth when we had a chance, though we constantly kept in touch.   It was odd of her to call me. I picked up and immediately thought the worst, like maybe something had happened to her baby girl, who was only a few months old at the time.

"Are you okay?" she asked me, her voice full of concern.

"Uh, yeah," I said, confused. I thought something was wrong with Cheslea or her baby, and she asked about me. Something wasn't right.

"Why?" I asked.

Her voice broke, "Oh my God. Destinee, where are you?"

"I'm going to the health department to get my COVID-19 vaccine. Why?"

"Oh my God. Pull over if you can." Her voice was cracking and painful.

I started shaking, and the tears welled up in my eyes. I could feel the tension of what was to come and was terrified.

"I'm getting ready to pull into the parking lot now," I said, putting on my blinker as I followed Jason's car in front of me. "Chelsea, what's wrong? You're scaring me." Something terrible was coming, but I couldn't imagine what it was.

"The Sheriff's Department published a report saying that Betty Facemyer, 61, of Sissonville, died in a car accident this morning. Your mom's last name was Facemyer, right?"

"Yeah," I said, trying to process it and make sense of it all as the news settled heavily in the pit of my stomach. That couldn't be right. It had to be the wrong person.

I pulled into the parking spot as reality crashed down around me.

"I've got to call Stella," I said, knowing that she probably didn't either if I didn't know. Chelsea apologized again and again for breaking the news to me. I got out of the car as Jason came around to open my door.

"I just got off the phone with Chelsea. Mom's dead." I said numbly, my fingers shaking as I searched for and quickly found that article confirming that. I couldn't believe it, yet there it was. In writing and published for the whole world to see:

By WSAZ News Staff

Published: Oct. 22, 2021 at 4:44 AM EDT

UPDATE 10/22/21 7:49 A.M.

BIG CHIMNEY, W.Va (WSAZ) – Kanawha County deputies have released the name of the person killed on Route 119 early Friday morning.

According to the Kanawha County Sheriff Department's Facebook post, [Betty Facemyer], 61 years old from Sissonville, West Virginia, was killed in the crash on Pennsylvania Avenue.

Deputies say Facemyer crossed the center line of the road and struck a pickup truck head on. Facemyer's dog was also in the car and died in the crash.

I dialed Stella's number, and when Rory answered, I just blurted out, "Mom's dead." No matter how often I said it, it wouldn't register in my head. She couldn't be dead, right? Maybe they could still bring her back to life. Perhaps they had the wrong person. Maybe there was another Betty Facemyer from the same area.

"What?" he said, sounding like he'd just woken up.

"I'm looking at it in the news right here," I said, reading him the published statement.

"Oh my God," he said, and then I heard him telling Stella in the background.

"I hate to jump off of here, but I need to go in and get my COVID shot," I said. I now realize I was running from the situation, thinking that if I could get back into the normalcy of life enough, it would reset everything, and Mom would still be here.

I put on my mask as tears dripped down my face in continuous streams. I couldn't stop them even if I wanted to. The grief of what I'd just lost settled in around me and threatened to suffocate me.

I sat in the waiting room as Jason helped me complete the paperwork. My brain couldn't make sense of the words on the paper. I felt like a stun grenade had just gone off in my life. My ears were ringing, everything and everyone seemed to move slowly around me, and noises were muffled. I was underwater, drowning in my grief.

"Are you okay?" one of the nurses asked me again as she sterilized the injection site. *How had I gotten here?* She still sounded muffled, but the repetition of her question brought me close enough to the surface of reality that I could understand.

"My mom just died. I just found out my mom just died." I said as tears continued to stream down my face. They offered me tissues, but I felt like no amount in the world would suffice to soak up the tears I knew would come from this crushing heartache.

I emailed work, letting them know I wouldn't be there that day. Luckily, it was a Friday, so I had the weekend to figure things out. I didn't even know where to start or what to do. I was so lost. I tried to make sense of what had happened. *Why had Mom been out at 4 a.m.? What had she been doing on her way to Elkview? Was she trying to kill herself?* Not knowing the circumstances surrounding her death was enough to drive me mad. I needed answers. I needed closure. I needed something. I needed my mom.

Stella called me back and explained that she'd spoken to the hospital and Abigail. The paramedics immediately recognized the name since Mom had been brought in so often after calling 911 when she couldn't breathe. Sadie's boyfriend was an EMT, so the news was passed directly to Sadie, and they counted that as telling an immediate family member and released the name to the press.

Sadie called Abigail, who had been trying to get ahold of Stella when I called her. Stella went on to explain that someone needed to claim her body, and we agreed that all three of us would do it that evening.

I had never gotten a normal relationship with Mom, and now I never would. She was gone, and any chance I had of normalcy had died with her. I hated that we were now referring to Mom as just a body. She was so much more than that. That was my mom. Despite her shortcomings and everything she said or did to me, that was my mom. I felt ashamed that I'd stonewalled her for so long. All that time was gone, and I would never get it back. She died thinking I hated her.

I called Mamaw Goldie that day, looking for guidance as to what to do. I'd never dealt with death so close to me before; our family was small, and we didn't often lose people. Instead of offering comfort or direction, she chose to berate me for not having helped Mom more while she was alive. It's like she was blaming me for Mom's death - for sending Mom over the edge and causing her to feel desolate enough to reach the point of hopelessness.

Mamaw went on to brag about all the things she and Gertie had done for Mom in the months leading up to her death - from paying her bills to getting her groceries and giving her money. She shamed me and my sisters for not doing the same.

I tried to explain to her that we all had families that were taking care of and we didn't have extra money to throw at her. She wouldn't listen to reason, though.

Stella, Abigail, and I met at the hospital that night to claim Mom's body and belongings so that we could start the process of laying her to rest, however we chose to do so. These were not choices I wanted to be making. All three of us banded together to support each other through it. We had Mom cremated as she didn't have life insurance or any money to cover the outrageous cost of a funeral. We split the cost between the three of us and got the free urn with the cremation.

Meanwhile, the landlord gave us a week to clean out Mom's apartment. I took off work that week to help Stella and Abigail grab whatever we could out of Mom's belongings. We sorted through boxes and totes of paperwork and pictures. While going through her closet, surrounded by her clothes and her scent, I broke down, knowing that I would never again be in her house or her closet, ever again. That chapter had closed, and I could never get it back.

On my way to work the following week, I remember being in awe that people were going about their daily lives like nothing had happened. I felt like I had suffered this great tragedy that had rocked my world to the equivalent of a natural disaster, and people were still carrying on about their business.

I wanted to scream at them to stop and see the damage from the wreckage. I again sank into the bottomless abyss that is depression. I couldn't get out of bed and lashed out at Jason. I maxed out my credit cards, buying senseless things I did not need to fill the void of what I'd just lost. We'd just recently gotten them all paid off. I lost control again and lost all of the progress I'd made in healing because I had this gashing wound that I couldn't get to stop bleeding and hurting.

I missed Mom so incredibly much - more than I could ever begin to put into words. Every time I tried, I started to cry. Her death had left me breathless, just as I'd been when she gave me life. I had no closure on all that I'd lost - the decades that I had lost and would never get back. It was confusing for me, too, because I felt like I'd already lost her once before - after I got taken away from her. She hadn't been gone, though, as I'd still seen her again in a different setting. I somehow couldn't wrap my mind around the fact that this was not the same - I wouldn't still see her in a different setting. She was gone and really gone this time. Forever.

Mamaw started talking about going to see Mom's body - there was that word again - at the funeral home so that she could see for herself that her eldest daughter was dead. Because we'd chosen to have Mom cremated, the funeral home didn't embalm her or anything, as that would be a waste of time and materials.

When we went to see Mom at the funeral home, she was lying on a gurney with a cloth mainly covering her. I only needed a glance at her to confirm what I already knew, while Gertie and Mamaw chose to examine her body more closely.

That was my mom's body, but that's it. That wasn't my mom. My mom's face wasn't that sunken in and that drained of life. Her nose was not that skinny and flat. I buried my face in Jason's shirt to erase the memory of what I'd just seen. He'd driven from work on that rainy day to support me during this process, and I couldn't have been more appreciative. I knew I didn't deserve it after all I'd put him through, but he still showed up when I needed him the most.

After our time was up, and we could no longer retrieve Mom's items from her apartment, the nightmares started. They were all similar, and the scenes were almost always the same. My sisters and I are cleaning Mom's apartment, desperately trying to grab anything deemed essential, anything we might miss, or anything that held sentimental value. In our grief, I knew that our mission was not completed successfully. I knew that we had left some stuff behind, our grief prohibiting us from digging too deep into the piles of junk. That part of my nightmare was always the same. Another part of my nightmare that was always the same was the inclusion of Mom, her body grey and decaying from death, sitting up in a chair while we worked around her.

Though I already knew the answer, I've researched what these dreams could mean. They're representative of someone struggling to accept death. They indicate someone who feels disconnected from a piece of oneself associated with the recently deceased. They point to the fact that a person has painful memories associated with the recently deceased that need to be worked through.

While I have had some material tendencies, there was no materialistic drive to get stuff out of Mom's apartment. It was only to have pieces of her: pictures of her I'd never seen before from when she was a young girl, her old Polaroid camera that I still use to this day, letters with her shaky yet familiar handwriting, and anything that held on to her scent. Along with all the mementos was a marble urn filled with John's ashes on Mom's coffee table. Because John had played the most significant role in my life, and because his son had said he didn't want them, I took John's ashes home with me until we decided what to do next. Once Mom was cremated, I kept her ashes beside John's so they'd still be together in death.

My pain was too intense for me to bear. I reached out to my church, desperate for guidance. My pastor, who was out of town then, put me in touch with a local church member who could mentor me through this.

I hadn't attended church like I should have, but started getting more involved. As time went on, I became closer and closer to the mentor from church. I joined the choir and a bible study group on Sunday mornings and evenings, but God wasn't working in my heart. I was doing it all to impress her, as I was too fearful to allow God to change me.

When my mentor started calling me out on living with a man and not being married, I made up lies about his situation to cover it up. I didn't want to be judged for how I was living, even though I knew it was against God's law. When she brought up how it was negatively impacting Sawyer – that he would learn my habits from me, I stopped going to church. I felt bullied, but it was due to a lack of responsibility on my part. I could no longer handle the weight of the perceived judgment from those I went to church with. It was my guilt and shame eating me alive.

Chapter Twenty-Seven: Mom Deserved Better

A year after Mom passed, I was told that we would be burying Mom and John together in a cemetery near Mamaw and Gertie. Gertie was paranoid that Judy, John's ex-wife, wanted to steal his ashes, which was a delusion born out of grief. Together, Gertie and Mamaw devised a plan to make the ashes unreachable. In the days leading up to the day we were going to bury the ashes, I found out the severity of their paranoia. They planned to dump both sets of ashes into a small metal trashcan, bury the trashcan at the chosen gravesite, and then cover it with concrete.

The idea of a gust of wind blowing while we poured Mom's ashes into a literal trashcan, along with the thought of those ashes getting all over everyone, was enough to make me want to vomit. I could not believe that they were willing to disrespect their daughter – their sister, *my mom* - like that. Unwilling to let Mom's remains be buried in a trashcan, and knowing that Gertie and Mamaw were not to be reasoned with, I devised a plan.

A quick Google search informed me that cremated human remains resemble almond flour in color and texture. So, after a quick trip to my local grocery store, I had the almond flour I needed. With Jason's help - since I couldn't bring myself to look at or handle Mom's remains - I switched out the bag of ashes for a Ziploc bag of almond flour, not caring if the brand-named bag gave me away. I let Stella and Abigail know what I was doing so that they would be aware of where Mom was laid to rest, too, since I couldn't allow them to disrespect her in such a way.

The day came, and I retrieved the urns from my car, ready to help Dale dump almond flour in a trashcan if it came down to it. Luckily, John's urn was much nicer than Mom's, and his urn was fused shut, thus rendering the ashes unreachable. I heaved a sigh of relief. Plans changed, and Gertie decided it was worth the risk to bury the urns in the ground. I switched the almond flour back for Mom's ashes, and we buried Mom's and John's ashes side by side, where they had both wanted to be in life and death. Gertie was adamant that they would need to cover the hole with concrete to keep Judy from digging them up. I wasn't sure where this paranoia with Judy came from; I'd never met or heard her mentioned before.

The grief of losing someone so close had gotten to Mamaw Goldie and Gertie, and the façade that had been so well-crafted for the world to see slipped away. And like most people who are hurting, they were seeking to hurt someone. They chose me.

Gertie and Mamaw started telling anyone who would listen that I had made plans with Judy so she could steal John's ashes. She'd started the gossip with Stella while we were at Mamaw's house, gathered together before we laid our loved ones to rest. Meanwhile, I'd never even met the woman - she was a part of John's life before I came into the picture. Before Stella had called and asked if I'd been talking with Judy, I wasn't even aware that such a person existed.

Gertie fabricated a story that I had switched out John's urn for a different one. She claimed that the urn that I had brought to Mamaw's to bury was not the same urn that John's ashes had been in initially, and she believed that I had sold John's ashes to Judy in a cheap attempt to make some money. None of which was true, but she could not be reasoned with. They continue to spread lies about my character to this day, but I've made peace with it. Hurt people hurt people.

Chapter Twenty-Eight: Repeating History

Mom's death rocked our relationship. It had set me back quite a bit. Jason, being ever the one to run away from his issues, especially with women, rather than face them and work through them, left or threatened to leave time and time again. I begged him to stay each time, feeling less like a person as the begging chipped away at my dignity. My fear of being abandoned because I was not deemed worthy was exacerbated. The only difference was that I now had a voice to convince him to stay, but my self-worth plummeted in the process.

Jason often made empty threats to leave because he "just couldn't do it anymore"; other times, I talked him into coming back. He was still hesitant to trust me, and I was still a ticking time bomb waiting to go off at any moment. We got married that January, three years after we started our affair. I'd learned from the last time that I wanted something simple. We didn't tell anyone in our families that we were getting married or when. We just got ready, took pictures, and then went to the courthouse and said our vows.

We'd come a long way in overcoming our pasts, but we still had so far to go. We fought constantly, our arguments lasting late into the night, and we were getting more comfortable crossing previously off-limits boundaries. For example, I slapped him one night even after I promised I wouldn't ever again, and he slapped me right back, chipping the tiniest part of my tooth.

As time went on, we were still making progress. I'd stopped focusing so much on my physical appearance and gotten rid of social media to gain cheap attention and validation from others. I was learning to be more in tune with my emotional state, though I still tended to let my anxiety get the best of me. I was on antidepressants and anti-anxiety medication, but neither of them seemed to be working because neither of them was getting to the root of my problems. They were simply acting as a band-aid, as had everything else. A band-aid that was frequently failing at its job to help me hold it together.

One evening, about a year into our marriage, Jason was imbibing in alcohol, which was his favorite way to cope when the kids weren't around. It was something he'd picked up in his early twenties to deal with the barrage of insults from his previous wife, and his dependence had gotten worse since we've been together.

Jason had had an incredibly stressful day at work, and I hadn't helped. I had had a dream the night before that he had cheated on me, which left me sensitive and vulnerable all day. He didn't have patience for my need for reassurance with everything else at work, but I pressed on, expecting his reassurance that he wasn't cheating on me, even though I already knew he wasn't. My insecurities and fears of someone else being chosen instead of me were still suffocating me. He soon grew tired of me and spent the evening gaming, escaping into games to relax, calm down from the day's stress, and get away from my nagging. When he came upstairs to talk to me, I could hear the slur in his speech from his heavy drinking and could sense the undercurrent of anger. I worried this would lead to another argument, as Jason tended to be unreasonable when he drank.

When he went back downstairs, I quietly snuck down there, grabbed his cup of alcohol, and locked the door so that he could play his game in peace. I no longer had to worry about his condition worsening. I was just trying to protect him and myself as peacefully as I saw fit. I worried he would throw a fit if I asked him to stop drinking that night. The anger was already radiating from him, and he hated being told "no".

My choice to take matters into my own hands had been a mistake, even though I had the best intentions. For Jason already had issues with female authority figures dictating his every move. When he came upstairs to address the issue of my taking his cup, he was unhappy and had no patience left. I accused him of being insensitive, and he accused me of trying to control him. He pressed his body against mine and glared down at me with hatred in his eyes to intimidate me. His six-foot figure towered over me by a good half a foot. I pushed him away, unwilling to let him see how badly he was scaring me.

He grabbed me by my throat, picked me up like I was a rag doll, and slammed me onto the floor. My head cracked against the laminate flooring, and for a moment, I felt nothing. Then the pain radiated up throughout my body and concentrated in my heart. I was stunned that this was happening.

I'd watched Mom and John fight dozens of times as a child, but I never imagined this would happen to me. I thought I'd done well to avoid being the stereotypical female in our lineage who let her husband beat on her. I wasn't any better than any of the rest of them.

I was terrified for my life, knowing that he wasn't using his full strength and that he had trained in martial arts as a teenager. It would be too easy for him. If he wanted to kill me, he could.

I'd never been enough to make anyone want to protect me or save me or love me thus far in life, and I doubted there was anything I could do to make him not kill me if he wanted to. I kicked and clawed my way away from him, leaving a massive gash on his face. I stared at him, scared, of course, but also deeply hurt. I'd developed this almost God-like complex about him – as if he was my savior who would come and fix all of my problems. He shattered my faith and trust in him to take care of me.

As we continued to argue, I brushed past him to get to the bedroom. He, again, took it as a personal attack, as was his modus operandi. He wrapped his long fingers around my neck again and slammed me into the wall in the hallway outside our bedroom door. The whole house shook as if to acknowledge my fear. I shoved my fingers into his eye socket until he let go.

When I tried to get away, swatting my hands at him the whole time in hopes of deterring his attack, he threw me to the ground and choked me. His hands gripped tighter around my throat with each passing second as he glared down at me with fury in his eyes. I never hated blue eyes more in my life.

As my vision blackened, I desperately reached for whatever I could, grabbing what I could of his genitalia and squeezing until he finally let go.

Flashes of Mom and John played in my head like rapid-fire; I was heartbroken again. He had been accused of putting his hands on his ex-wife and had sworn to me that it had never happened. He assured me that was not who he was. I had believed him. Now, I wasn't so sure. He'd told me horror stories about his ex-wife and all that she had put him through, and I couldn't imagine that anything that I'd done had been any worse, any more deserving of this torment.

I cried and begged him to leave that night, my whole body trembling with terror and PTSD, feeling that there was no way to move past this. How would I ever be able to look him in the eyes again? How would I ever feel safe in his arms again? How would I ever not flinch when he went to touch me? The words "if he does it once, he'll do it again" rang in my head.

He insisted that I call the cops, as that was the only way he would leave. I couldn't bring myself to. I couldn't allow history to repeat itself with Sawyer's stepdad dragged away in handcuffs for beating up his mom. I couldn't live with myself knowing that if I called the cops, Jason would most definitely lose his job and the right to see his kids. It would ruin his life. As much as he'd hurt me, I couldn't bring myself to do the same to him.

Later that night, after things had finally calmed down, he sobered up, and we were able to talk; the realization of what had happened settled upon me. And him. I felt so incredibly close to Mom, and I felt a renewed love and appreciation for her. I valued her strength in fighting back with John as hard and often as she did. I had only done it one night, and I was terrified. That was enough for me. But that was her life. For years, she had quite literally fought to stay alive. My heart broke for her again as I realized how painful and scary that must have been for her.

I'm not going to lie and tell you that staying was an easy choice because it wasn't. I still struggle to reconcile it to this day, and Jason always tells me that he thinks I should have left. Since then, there have been other women in my family who have experienced domestic abuse, not quite to the same level, but abuse nonetheless, and like a hypocrite, I beg them to leave their spouses.

There's nothing I can say to justify my staying or what Jason did because there is no justification. What I can tell you is that that experience broke open whatever was preventing me from healing from my past. So many pieces of the confusing and disheveled puzzle that is my life started to click into place, and things slowly started to make sense.

It began with understanding Mom more and not only appreciating her efforts, even though they didn't seem like much from the outside, but also showing her grace. I understood where she came from and why she did what she did, and I realized that Mom was doing her best. I extended that same grace to Jason and worked to understand his actions rather than judge his behavior.

After he attacked me, I stopped working out. One reason is that I began to hate myself more because I equated his actions with his hating me. The second reason is that I wanted to work on my mental and emotional growth, which eventually gave way to spiritual growth after I answered God's calling and drew closer to Him. Lastly, I realized that no matter how physically strong I was, it would not make a difference if he attacked me again. He would always be bigger and stronger than me. My trust in him to protect me was shattered that day and I never quite got it back.

Jason and I tried to heal from this. I'd grown tired of running from my problems when things got difficult or uncomfortable, and I forced myself to face my mistakes. Jason didn't have a sip of alcohol after that night out of respect for my fears. He claims it wasn't the alcohol that made him do that, but I stand by my belief that his inhibitions wouldn't have been compromised to that point had he not been drinking. He tried to reconcile the idea that I was not controlling him by disallowing his alcohol consumption, which is again linked to the unhealed trauma of his childhood.

Before Jason and I started our journey through life together, I'd been too ashamed of myself and my past to be self-aware. My shame was so great that I couldn't even stand to look at myself in any capacity because I hated what I saw. Jason worked to call me out on what I was doing wrong, and though I was not at all receptive to it at first, I eventually came to realize he was not doing it to be mean.

There were still times during arguments that I saw anger flash in his eyes, and I instinctively backed myself against the wall, preparing for the assault that I was sure will come. It hasn't come since that night, but still, I waited on it.

Chapter Twenty-Nine: But There Was Jesus

A few months later, I was lying in bed after having taken my usual antihistamine to help me have a chance of falling asleep. Without it, my anxieties would have kept me up all night. As I rolled over to go to sleep, my heart started to pound in my chest. Panicked, I sat up, feeling a numbness creep over my body. It was the numbness in my face that worried me. I smiled and relaxed repeatedly, frantically feeling my face with my clammy and shaky hands. It was all in my head, but I convinced myself that the left side of my face wasn't moving.

"I think I'm having a stroke," I said to Jason, the terror gripping me and making it more difficult to breathe with each passing second. Jason, ever the calm to my storm and my sense of logic when I get too emotional, gave me a once-over, asked me to smile, and indicated that it was false.

The fear that I had of having a stroke was replaced with this deep and despairing feeling of being separated from God, like, wholly and forever separated as I would be in the fiery pits of hell. I'd dealt with abandonment my whole life, so it was something I'd become familiar with. But the sense of abandonment I felt that night was unlike anything I'd ever experienced. At the time, I couldn't even put it into words – all I knew was that it terrified me. Then this sinking feeling came over me that if I died that night, even though I had said the words to accept Jesus into my heart, and I'd always claimed and honestly believed I would, I would not get into heaven. The realization shook me to my core.

Over the following days, I would learn to articulate my experience and how it sparked a change within me. I now believe that this was an undeniable wake-up call from God. He had allowed me to go through my challenges for a reason – He can use all things for His good after all. But I was not on the path that He had destined for me. I was, in and because of my hurt, hurting others around me – projecting and inflicting the same pain I'd endured on others. That's not what God had intended – I was not walking in His purpose. I was leaning on my own understanding and refusing to acknowledge His direction.

For the duration of my life, even though I claimed to be a Christian and wore a Christian face for everyone to see, I couldn't bring myself to let go of the hurt. I carried around so much shame for years, feeling like I'd somehow deserved what had happened to me, which I now realize is a normal trauma response for people.

I didn't have faith in God to wash it all away because I felt so unlovable, even by the one who loved me so much He gave His life to save me. After the complete separation I felt from Jesus that night, I began to see my pain for what it was. I realized I couldn't hide from Jesus, no matter how hard I tried. As the layers peeled back, God showed me the sad, scared, lonely little girl who was still stuck trembling with fear and abandonment after the injustice that had been done.

Realization clicked into place for me as I came to understand that I didn't deserve any of what had happened to me - I wasn't worthless or too broken to be deserving of good things. I wasn't a bad person because of how anyone's pain had hurt me. It was then that the dam broke, and grief flowed in for that little girl whom I'd lost so long ago - the one so full of life and love that she couldn't contain it. She continued to pour her love out to others instead of saving any for herself because she didn't feel like she was good enough to deserve it, and for the first time in my life, I allowed myself to grieve. I grieved for all that I'd lost and all that was taken from me. I grieved for the years I'd wasted hurting.

I felt like Adam and Eve did in the Garden of Eden when their Creator exposed their sins. I looked up to the heavens, exposing my brokenness to God, desperate for answers and salvation. Rather than be critical of the challenges I'd experienced or the mess I'd made of my life, as I was so terrified He would be, Jesus met me with nothing but love. It was the overwhelming, all-encompassing, unconditional love I had longed for my entire life. It was the love I should have received from my parents and anyone who stepped in to take on that role. And just like in Jericho, all those thousands of years ago, all my walls and inhibitions came tumbling down, and God's eternal love rushed in. I heard Him say, "I've got you, My child." And I let the beautiful, awe-inspiring healing begin.

I've still got a long road of healing ahead of me, but I'm now willing to move forward with it, whereas before, I was too scared of what I'd find if and when I started to uncover the damage and hurt. I still struggle sometimes with what my counselor calls "stinkin' thinkin'" which is that voice in my head that tells I'm not worthy of love or that I'll never be enough. I'm learning to rely on scripture to counteract that so that I am reassured that God does love me, sees me as worthy, and thinks that I'm enough, even when I don't believe it myself.

That's not to say that I'm now a perfect person or think of myself as a perfect person by any means – which is a common misconception about Christians from the secular worldview. I don't think I'm above anyone for having found Christ. I know that I am flawed and weak, and that's the whole reason I work so hard to surrender to Christ completely. I realize that I can't do this on my own. I've proven that to myself a few too many times. I also recognize that I sin and fall short of the glory of God every single day, but I am saved through God's grace. I followed the world and hated myself all the more for it. Now, I seek to follow the Lamb wherever He goes.

My trauma and my inability to process said trauma wrecked me, as is evident from my life choices and my constant search for something to fill the voids that were left in the wake of my tragedy. After Mom had tried to kill me, nobody ever explained or helped me process the series of unfortunate events that were my life. The protection and security that is necessary for a child to develop correctly was ripped out from under me, and I struggled to find my footing. For a long time, I felt like I'd been left behind - I was stuck in the mindset of myself as a four-year-old - stuck trying to process what had happened to me while the rest of the world moved on without me and seemingly, despite me.

Though I was placed with various families throughout the years, I choose to pack up and leave when I realized I would not fit in. This fight-or-flight response stemmed from the trauma that I'd endured. No matter how hard I tried to conform and change myself, I would never adhere to what anyone wanted me to be.

This constant changing of myself to be what everyone else wanted me to be inhibited me from developing my sense of identity – not that I had a firm foundation on which to establish one, anyway. I turned to others' expectations of me and celebrities I looked up to for help in becoming someone worthy of love. The only thing I *was* sure of about myself was that my mom had tried to kill me and that my dad had left me, so that became my foundation on which I built my identity. The message from both events was clear: I wasn't loved. Because it was the only conclusion I could draw with my narrow perspective, I convinced myself that I was unlovable and undeserving of anyone's love. Because I was convinced that the two people who were supposed to love me more than anything in the world hated me, I began to hate myself. So much so that any critique or comment about my negative behavior became a devastating blow to my already-sensitive ego and sense of worth.

Even so, I'd grown up attending church – learning and singing about God's love. I'd heard testimonies of people around me about how God's love had changed them and made them better people. I'd seen it happen. But, as much as I believed in the birth, life, death, burial, and resurrection of our Lord and Savior Jesus Christ, I did not have an ounce of faith in Him. Even the devil believes in Jesus, so it wasn't like my belief was something revolutionary. Of course, He exists; the evidence was all around me in creation and in all the ways He'd intervened to save me throughout my life, so there was no denying that.

I'd become aware that my experiences had led me to have severe trust issues, which is to be expected. But I honestly believed I was a good

Christian—I was doing everything I thought I should to look the part. I went to church, sang hymns, and prayed to God when I needed something. I did everything right—except trust in Jesus.

Even though I wasn't aware of it, I struggled to trust Him because many people had let me down. My trust in people to protect me and do what was best for me was destroyed. My experiences changed me and tainted every part of who I was becoming, taking over my entire being. My trauma was the one consistent thing in my life, so I clung to it, refusing to let go. I feared what I would find under the layers and layers of tragedy. It was easier to forge forward, put on a brave face, and pretend that I was unscathed. I'd tried every avenue possible to try to cure the symptoms of my mental and emotional unrest.

I tried various substances, I tried over-eating, I tried starving myself, I tried being lazy, I tried being overly active and busy, I tried therapy and breathing techniques, and I tried indulging in anything and anyone I wanted. I tried distracting myself with books, movies, social media, and video games. Doctors put me on an array of antidepressants - everything that society suggests to help people heal, I tried. My life had become a constant and despondent search for relief from my emotional suffering, which had time and again proven to be futile.

I was looking in all the wrong places, but I didn't realize it. Nothing is worse than being so lost that you're unaware of how lost you are. God had proven His goodness to me by protecting me all my life, but I didn't see it. I couldn't focus on anything except my hurt.

Because I felt like I was never good enough, I've often felt this need to improve or chase perfection constantly. I became a people-pleaser to a fault, needing someone to accept me. Sometimes, that's taken the form of academic success and accolades to impress others. I've pursued physical fitness and all but killed myself trying to achieve what I thought was the perfect body.

I'd grown up having media of various sorts program into my mind that the best way to get a man's attention was through physical attraction, and for a long time – that's all that I felt I had to offer.

I've had to realize I have a beautiful heart outside my beautiful face. It was the easiest and most shallow way to get the attention I craved. I needed someone to see me for all the brokenness, but I was ashamed to let anyone in. I was mortified by what they'd find – what I'd find – if anyone dared uncover the poison that had rotted my entire being.

I was mean to other kids in elementary school because I was so insecure and felt very much like I didn't belong, and I wanted to make sure other people felt that way, too.

In middle school, I was so eager to fit in that I morphed into whomever I was hanging around. I preferred to pursue boys' attention, which continued into high school.

I'm trying every day to learn from what I've come from so that I can leave the past behind. I'm learning to be okay with sitting with my pain and what I see in myself. I have to convince myself that my tendencies don't make me a bad person, they're just a response to the trauma that I endured. I have to convince myself that I didn't deserve anything that happened to me.

It's hard for me to accept love from people because I feel like I don't deserve it. It's hard for me to get rid that "stinkin' thinkin'," wherein my internal dialogue tries to convince me I'm still not deserving of good.

I'm working to instead remember that I am a daughter of the King. I am a princess in His eyes.

I've also had to come to terms with the fact that I don't know it all. My whole life, I've been let down by the people I trusted, so I stopped putting my trust in people. I flailed blindly through my life in my twenties, trying to figure it out without knowing what I was doing or where I was going. But nobody could reason with me – nobody could tell me otherwise. I couldn't accept the possibility that I might be wrong in how I was doing things.

The lack of acknowledgment of pain has allowed this pain to be passed down. I tried doing what they wanted me to do by keeping my head down and trudging through the mess. I tried to ignore the trauma and the damage, hoping that it would go away on its own. I only proved to myself time and again that was no way to live – I felt the unrest in my soul. It was like trying to hold in a scream that was fighting to get out. I realized I couldn't do it alone, and don't have to.

I've got God on my side, and the healing I've experienced through Him is giving me the strength, courage, and guidance to end the generational trauma. It stops here.

I may not have grown up with parents of my own the way that children usually do, but I'm breaking generational curses nonetheless. I pour love unashamedly and unconditionally into my son. He never doubts how dearly he is loved. Like him, I am a child of God. I have always been; I just had to realize it for myself. Looking back over my life, I see God's hand in everything. There was another in the fire with me the whole time. It is only by His grace and goodness that I have survived. I had to be completely broken and without hope – as if life hadn't stripped me of that enough – to realize how desolate I am without Him. Just like I had to delve into His Word to see the evidence of His love and recognize it in my own life, by His grace, I now see that generational curses don't stop just because you refuse to look at the damage. The symptoms will inevitably crop up, the trauma will be passed on, and the victims will continue their desperate and unfulfilling search for healing. Only by facing the pain, seeing it for what it is, and acknowledging what it's done to the family can change.

I've opened my heart and believe He can use what happened to me for good. Any searches for healing in the mundane and the carnal are futile and will lead to nothing but an insatiable desire to consume more.

The thirst is unquenchable and can only be satiated by the Living Water that is Jesus Christ. I'd grown to resent my grief, as I was so tired of hurting and feeling weak. Everyone else around me seemed to have it so easy, but every day was a struggle for me to stay alive. I still sometimes struggle to find reasons to live. Can you blame me? One of the first things I ever remember learning was how to kill myself. But I take those days in stride and show myself the grace Jesus extends to me daily.

I wish I could tell you that my life has gotten easier and that I no longer struggle with the ghosts of my past, but that would be a lie. There are days when my depression still threatens to swallow me whole, and I isolate myself from those around me so the pain doesn't leak out onto them. There are days when I miss my mom so much that I can't breathe as I long to have someone I can turn to and not feel like a burden.

There are difficult choices that I have to make to protect my son from the world as much as possible – something that many people around me don't understand. Call it hypervigilance, call it a trauma response, call it PTSD if you will. I call it showering him with love and

protection. I call it being the mom I should have had and breaking

generational curses.

Chapter Thirty: Destinee's Destiny

The thing that I struggle with the most is this deep sense of self-hatred. I've constantly got this voice in my head telling me I'm worthless, I'll never be enough, I'm a burden to everyone around me, and nobody loves me. As I work with my counselor, we are overwriting these negative thoughts with biblical verses that prove I'm precious in God's eyes. I often relish in the fact that Jesus thought I was so precious that He purposefully sought me out that night He scared me into putting my faith into Him – He wanted my heart that badly. I've spent my life chasing the love and attention of boys to no avail – only to be turned away and let down. The fact that the Creator of the universe actively called me out shows just how precious I am in His eyes and His heart. That's enough for me.

In the year after God's wake-up call for not walking in His purpose, I've grown closer to God and become more centered, and Jason seemed to grow angrier and more resentful toward me. This is normal for a marriage that is unequally yoked, as the devil seems to tighten his grip on the unbeliever while the believer draws closer to Jesus. That doesn't change the fact that it greatly damaged any solid foundation on which we tried to build our marriage.

While I tried to also help Jason heal from the pain I caused by showing him God's goodness and grace, all he could see was the bad from before. I'd read somewhere that it takes up to two years of changed behavior from the one who caused the pain for a person to heal from the emotional or mental pain. A lot of people hold on to pain and wear it as armor in order to protect themselves from getting hurt again rather than forgiving and letting go. Jason had this tendency as well as a desire to "heal" on his own. But, his healing process includes utilizing Band-Aids – alcohol, nicotine, vegging out with games and video reels – instead of doing the hard work required to heal. Jason's inability to see past the bad forced me to continue looking back at things about myself that I was desperate move past. This inhibited me from digging up the roots of self-hatred and resting in God's love. Every step I took forward in healing and loving myself, Jason's inability and unwillingness to heal dragged me back down. Because of his distrust of women and his inability to forgive, all the things I'd done wrong held so much more weight in his mind than any of the good I'd ever done and the scales were tipping.

After months of dealing with this, I was exhausted. Then, when doing what was best for my son meant a change of jobs and potential financial circumstances, rather than support me and stand by me as my husband, Jason told me he was going to divorce me. I scrambled to find some work to make him happy, and things calmed down for a while. But then Jason's fear and unwillingness to support me and our family reared its ugly head and any foundation we'd built was shattered.

This was a rollercoaster of emotions for not only both of us, but also the kids. When my counselor explained to me that this was not resting in God's perfect peace as He intends for His children, I realized that I needed to take a huge step of faith. As much as it hurt me, as much as it hurt Sawyer, and as much as it hurt Jason's kids, I decided to give in to his wishes to divorce me. I'd spent years trying to convince him I was worth staying for, and I had nothing to show for it. We weren't showing our kids what their future relationships should look like because ours was so poisonous. I couldn't, in good conscience, continue to hold on to something that was hurting me and our kids so badly.

Immediately, my brain wanted to fall into the old familiar mindset of feeling like a failure. I had rushed into a relationship, looking to find myself and had been let down yet again. The familiar thoughts of *I'm not good enough, no one will ever love me, I'll never be worthy of anything good* creeped into my mind, and I knew that I would buckle under the weight of them. But then, all of those negative feelings were replaced with a stunning realization: even if I wasn't enough for one man, I'm enough for God; even if one man doesn't love me, God does. All this time, I've worried about being enough for people, or being enough for God, only to realize that I was not allowing God's love and grace to be enough for me. I've had to overwrite all of the negative thoughts I've allowed myself to believe with truth from God's word. It hasn't been an easy process, this letting go of the things – the painful thoughts – I was so comfortable holding onto. But I know that my best days are, in fact, of ahead of me.

I don't know what the future holds for me now, but I know who holds my future, and that is enough. The same God who carefully crafted each mountain, meticulously designed each grain of sand, and diligently hung each and every star chose to bring me into this world and, against all odds, fought to keep me here. That's not for nothing. God's got big plans for me – a destiny that far surpasses anything I could ever come up with on my own.

EPILOGUE

I'm not entirely healed yet and might never be completely healed. The hurt was so intense and such a huge part of me that it left a deep wound. But I'm learning to embrace it and not be bitter about it anymore. I don't allow it to define who I am in God's eyes anymore.

The thing I've learned about healing is that there's no way around it; you've got to trudge through it to get out on the other side. It's messy and painful and might sometimes seem downright impossible, but it's so worth it. Healing is not linear – it's not a brisk uphill climb to summit the mountain – it's going to consist of a series of setbacks. I have to remind myself not to lose heart because the view from the top will take my breath away, I know. Future me is counting on current me to face those giants and do the hard work for a better, brighter future.

As I look back on my life, there's no denying God's hand in every step along the way. God was with me that night when Mom was trying to hurt me – He was with me as Mom called her friend to tell her what she was doing. He was with me, making sure her friend answered and cared enough to intervene. He was with me on that hill, protecting me from Ralph. God has been with me this whole time, waiting for me to notice His presence. I just had to slow down and stop focusing on the storm around me so that I could walk on the water with Him.

On this healing journey, God showed me how beautiful and intimate it is to connect with Him in my grief and with others. This connection is unique to His children earthside, as we will thankfully no longer experience grief in heaven. I've had to trudge through the trenches of my despair and acknowledge uncomfortable truths about myself, but it has been a beautiful experience nonetheless.

It's then that I realize that, despite everything I'd gone through during my life – all the pain and shame I'd accumulated – God could still use it for good. I don't have to hide or morph myself into something I'm not to be accepted.

If it meant that I could experience God's grace and love on this level, and it meant that I would bear this cross a thousand more times to protect Sawyer, I would relieve every aspect of life without question. I know God is going to use me and my circumstances for good. I know Sawyer will never have to endure what I did. I am at peace, walking in God's destiny.

Lost people around me who have witnessed the changes within me are convinced I'm suffering from a religious psychosis since I've given my life to Christ. The truth is I know crazy - I've seen crazy. I've stared crazy in the eyes as it almost killed me. I've been crazy. This isn't crazy. This is the sanest and clearest-headed I've ever been. I've spent my whole life feeling buried under the mess of my life, but I now realize

God was just planting me. Now, I get to blossom.

THANK YOU:

First, I want to thank my Lord and Savior, Jesus Christ, without whom I would not exist. I live and breathe today because He intervened. I trust in His purpose for my life – even when it takes some convincing on my part.

Thank you to Sawyer for making me a mommy and helping me realize that unconditional love does exist. Thank you for being the boy with the biggest heart. Your love for Jesus gives me hope that I, too, can have a child-like faith in our Creator.

Thank you to Chelsea for sticking with me through all the drama and turmoil. You're a real one – the most loyal friend I could have ever asked for.

Thank you to Debbie Jordan, who has spent hours on the phone with me, reminiscing about Mom. She stepped in to take care of me, and Mom, more times than I could ever possibly count.

Thank you to Neva, the woman who saved my life. I would not be here today had you not answered Mom's call that night.

Thank you to Tammy and Kevin for taking me in and loving me after the most traumatizing day of my life.

Thank you to my aunt and uncle for taking me in and trying your best to love me – I know my stubborn and feisty spirit did not make it easy. You always made it a point to treat all three of us girls as equally as possible.

Thank you to "Stella and Rory" for getting me the help I desperately needed and for giving me the best shot at life with a good education. Thank you, especially, to Stella, for loving me like her own baby when I was younger. I don't know that I would have survived without you.

Thank you to Amanda – your honesty is unmatched. I can't wait for you to tell your story.

Thank you to my niece, "Harper". Those late nights with you when we were teenagers saved my life. I'm sorry my pain had such a negative impact on you and your sisters.

Thank you to Robert and Joyce for treating me like one of your own grandchildren and your support through my recent struggles. Joyce, thank you for reading my massive undertaking of a book and offering your expertise as a retired English teacher.

Thank you to "Jason" – the first person to ever really see me. And for teaching me how to start loving myself. Thank you for so many long talks about my book – changing and adding things – and for reading it more times than I can count. You probably know it almost as well as I do by now.

Thank you to "Tessa and Jake" for taking me in when I had

nowhere to go and for taking such good care of Sawyer.

Thank you to "Easton" for giving me Sawyer.

Thank you to every other village member who has had a hand in getting me where I am today – you stepped into a role you didn't have to and I know I was not easy to deal with.

Thank you to my counselor, Joyce, for helping me overwrite decades worth of "stinkin' thinkin'" as I realize how precious I am in God's eyes and step into His purpose.